Wheeling Matilda

The Story of Australian Cycling

by
Jim Fitzpatrick

STAR HILL
STUDIO

Published in Australia in 2013
by Star Hill Studio Pty Ltd
ABN 12 135 353 249
342 Mt. Kilcoy Road,
Kilcoy, Queensland, 4515, Australia

Telephone: 61 7 54981364
www.starhillstudio.com.au

© Star Hill Studio Pty Ltd 2013

All rights reserved.
No part of this publication may be reproduced,
stored in a retrieval system, or transmitted,
in any form or by any means without
the permission of the publisher.

ISBN 978-0-9871437-1-6

National Library of Australia
Cataloguing-in-Publication entry
Author: Fitzpatrick, Jim, 1943- author.
Title: Wheeling Matilda: the story
of Australian cycling / Jim Fitzpatrick.
ISBN: 9780987143716 (paperback)
Notes: Includes bibliographical references and index.
Subjects: Cycling--Australia--History.
Cyclists--Australia--History.

Dewey Number: 796.6

To my sons.

Contents

Preface	1
Introduction	2
'Bicycling'	3
The Country	3
The Machines	5
1. The Early Years	8
The High Wheelers	8
The Safety Bicycle	11
1893 – The Landmark Year	14
2. Western Australia	16
The Westralian Niche	18
The Cycling Telegraph	22
Camel Pads	27
The Goldfields Bicycle Pad Protection League	29
3. Maps, Guides and English	34
Road Maps and Guides	35
The Australian Alps	40
The Bicycle and Australian English	44
4. The Overlanders	48
The Trans-Nullarbor	49
Across the Centre	55
Around the Continent	59
Francis Birtles	66
Donald Mackay	71
Ted Ryko/Eddie Reichenbach	81
5. The Humble Tool	88
The Eastern Colonies	89

The Shearers	90
The Western Australian Rabbit Fence	92
Kalgoorlie Pipeline Lengthrunners	96
Kangaroo Shooting and Timber Cutting	97
The Decline of Rural Use	98
Pedal Power	101
The Tyres	102
6. The Bicycle at War	**104**
The Boer War	104
The Military Relay Rides	109
World War I	114
The ANZAC Cyclist Battalions	116
The Invasion of Malaya-Singapore	121
The Australian Home Front	125
Vietnam	129
7. A Racing Powerhouse	**134**
Major Taylor in Australia	139
Aussies Abroad	146
The Modern Powerhouse	149
Drugs	158
8. The Australian Legend	**160**
9. The Bicycle Today	**166**
The Better Life	169
From Marginal to Mainstream	172
Advocacy	174
Helmets	175
Conclusion	177
Acknowledgements, Sources and Bibliography	180
Illustrations	187
Index	190

Preface

As most Australians know, a 'matilda' is a swag, bag or rolled up blanket containing one's personal belongings, provisions and so on. It was carried by rural workers such as sheep shearers going about their routine business, or by itinerant swagmen who tramped the roads seeking work or simply a meal in exchange for odd jobs. During the severe depression of the 1890s men walked great distances across the vast rural landscape, carrying their swags, or 'waltzing matilda'.

The advent of the modern safety bicycle changed the game. The machine revolutionised urban and rural travel and life, and by 1893 numerous bushies and others were pedalling about the countryside.

Wheeling Matilda looks at the varied nature and extent of bicycle use by Australians in the bush, in the cities, in wartime, in cycle racing and for touring and travel—both past and present, and at home and abroad.

This book revisits thirty-five years of research into Australian cycling history and commentary on the bicycle's present-day use. It is intended to refresh old memories, and inform new ones.

I trust you enjoy reading it as much as I have enjoyed researching and writing it.

Jim Fitzpatrick
Kilcoy, Queensland
Australia
September 2013

Introduction

The island continent of Australia and the bicycle seem almost to have been made for one another.

Among other things, from 1893 the machine was adopted over the next two decades for more varied uses, and was routinely ridden over greater distances as part of daily rural life, than anywhere else on earth. At the turn of the 20th century, cycle racing—centred in Europe and North America—was the most popular, lucrative and widely followed sport internationally. Yet, half a world away, Australia sponsored the world's richest race and still hosts the oldest continuous track race and second oldest road race in existence. Today the small population (23,000,000) produces some of the top riders on the international racing scene and hosts The Tour Down Under, the opening event of the annual UCI racing calendar. The bicycle saw its

General store at Bullfinch, Western Australia, circa 1895

first significant military use during the Boer War (1899-1902), in which experienced Australian bush cyclists demonstrated the machine's wartime value. And to top it all off, by 1896 there was an extensive—and well used—bicycle path network in Western Australia that linked communities over an area the equivalent of Arizona and southern Utah (or Germany and Denmark) combined.

It is a remarkable cycling history.

'Bicycling'

The concept of 'bicycling' is fundamental to understanding the role of the machine in Australia (and elsewhere). A cyclist is not a person on wheels, but a person with wheels. There is an immense difference. While 'riding a bicycle' is the usual image, bicycling is essentially a man-machine combination that allows mode to be matched to terrain, optimising the use of wheel and foot. When sand, mud, obstacles, high winds, or a steep incline make pedalling difficult, the rider can get off and walk. The cycle can be pushed, carried, lifted over fences and floated across rivers. Heavy weights and bulky loads can be transported on it. Moreover, man and machine can be readily carried on wagons, trucks, cars, boats, or trains. It was that combination that radically altered the human travel equation in the 1890s.

The Country

When the modern safety bicycle arrived on the Australian scene in the late 1880s the country had only been occupied for a century by Europeans, mostly from the British Isles. Australia is the size of America's contiguous forty-eight states, but the majority of its three million residents lived within two hundred miles of the eastern and southeastern coastline, with most people centred about a few coastal cities (Sydney and Melbourne combined accounted for a third of the total). Beyond the few small inland towns of note, the eastern third of the continent was the province of sparsely distributed agriculturalists, pastoralists, miners, and keepers of telegraph stations and government outposts. The western two-thirds of Australia, among the hotter and more arid places on earth, was mostly unsettled.

Only a handful of explorers had crossed it; their accounts of it suggested no reason for others to follow, and few did. In fact, the second largest lake in Australia, which would rank in area behind the Great Lakes and the Great Salt Lake in America, was only discovered by aerial survey in 1932.

Aboriginal man was confined to walking. Early Europeans brought with them the horse, bullock, donkey and later, camels (from circa 1860). These allowed them to move themselves and large amounts of goods across the countryside but the rate of travel was not substantially increased. When introduced the energy-efficient bicycle was not only much faster across the countryside than a pedestrian, horse or camel, but could carry the rider and substantial additional weight in the process, and was not restricted to formed roads or tracks. The fact that it did not need food or water or eat poisonous plants and die, as did horses and camels, was no mean asset in drought-prone Australia.

The climate over most of Australia permits year-round cycling. Although summers can be extremely hot in some regions (think of Phoenix, Arizona), the winters are generally mild. There is no snow or ice to contend with other than in a few settled areas in the southeast, and even in most of those communities only occasionally. Of great importance, much of the continent

Sydney Cricket Ground, with cycle track on the oval perimeter

is relatively flat—three-quarters lies between 600 and 1,500 feet (183 and 457 m) above sea level, and only five per cent is over 2,000 feet (609 m). The highest peak is only 7,310 feet (2,228 m). Also, there are no political, linguistic or social barriers to movement.

Only a few railway lines existed even in settled areas (and none over some three-quarters of the country), and inland water transport was essentially limited to the Murray-Darling River system in the southeast. That left vast spaces to be crossed by walking, riding a horse, travelling by horse-drawn vehicle, or (to a very minor extent) using a camel. Rural workers such as shearers, rouseabouts, prospectors, commercial travellers, ministers and others who served the scattered population were perennially on the move, often walking between various properties and mining centres. Teamsters and carting contractors routinely trod thousands of miles annually alongside their bullock or horse teams or pack camels.

The perception of time, distance, travel and work was very different from today, and can probably only be fully appreciated by those totally and irrevocably confined within its framework. 'Thirty miles from tree to tree does not seem much in a motor car, but padding the hoof is a different matter especially under a burning sun'. I am aware of no other country at the time in which so many people travelled so far as part of their work routine. Australia was a land truly amenable to bicycling and the machine quickly proved itself a superb personal transport device and godsend for many.

The Machines

The safety bicycle (so named because it was much safer to ride than earlier models) was a technological marvel. The deceptively delicate-looking device encompassed such recent innovations as the ball bearing, tubular steel frame, roller bearing chain, tangentially spoked wheel and pneumatic tyre—all invented during the course of cycle development. The bicycle was lightweight and proved strong, durable, reliable and capable of operating with a minimum of maintenance. Although the product of some advanced manufacturing processes, any reasonably competent handyman could assemble and repair it. Of great importance, the bicycle could, where necessary, function with makeshift repairs.

Wheeling Matilda

Boer War cycle troops

Through the 1890s the bicycles of Australian city dwellers and rural travellers alike were basic diamond frame roadster machines (with drop frames for women), steel, about 27 pounds (12.3 kg), a single gear, fixed wheel, and as likely as not to have no brake (riders slowed by resisting the forward motion of the pedal). Handlebars were pivoted at the headset, with little or no vertical height adjustment and no gooseneck to allow forward or backward adjustment until 1903. Riders generally rode upright on a well-sprung seat to minimise fatigue, soreness, and injury from long hours and rough surfaces. Standard roadster tyres were common but many rural travellers relied upon Dunlop's Thorn-Proof tyres, developed partly as a result of Australia's needs. They were thicker, more rigid, and heavier to pedal but minimised punctures in a country with numerous thorny plants.

Travellers (especially rural workers) often carried considerable weight on their bicycles. Luggage was initially secured on the handlebars and within the frame, as fixed wheel riders tended to keep the rear wheel clear for a safe dismount if they lost control of rapidly spinning pedals. By 1900 freewheels with backpedal brakes were coming into use, enabling much bulkier loads to be carried over the rear wheel. Fifty to seventy-five pounds (23 - 34 kg) was common and sometimes much more (one imperial gallon weighs ten pounds (4.5 kg) and waterbags hung under the crossbar were a standard item for rural travel). Cyclists rode on everything from beautifully smooth dry lake beds, clay pans and camel pads to rough roads, mere bush tracks, and natural surfaces of sand, gravel, stones, mud and clay. They also pushed and, where necessary, picked up the machine and its load and carried it—whatever it took to get wherever they were going.

Ted Catchlove, Arltunga, Northern Territory, 1903

The Early Years

Advances in overseas cycle technology were quickly introduced to Australia as an intense interest in cycling matters developed and was maintained by a cadre of tourists, racers, clubs and commercial interests. In 1867 a velocipede was built in New South Wales, half a decade after its invention in Europe. The first one was apparently introduced to Melbourne in 1868 and Australia's first bicycle race was held the following July at the Melbourne Cricket Ground, although some claimed that there had already been 'contests' in Sydney in 1867.

The High Wheelers

A velocipede tricycle at Clarendon, South Australia, date unknown

Australia's first cycling boom was occasioned by the introduction of the high wheeler or penny-farthing cycles (also known as ordinaries), with Melbourne the premier centre. The first high wheeler in Australia was imported into

Melbourne in 1875. Adherents eventually formed the Melbourne Bicycle Club in 1878, the Sydney Bicycle Club in 1879, a Tasmanian club in 1880, and South Australian and Brisbane bicycle clubs in 1881. Western Australia's first club was not formed until the late 1880s; it folded soon thereafter and was eventually superseded by the W.A. Cycling Club in 1891. High wheeler cycle clubs were established in some rural communities as early as 1886 and they could be found in surprising locations, such as the relatively remote communities of Charleville and Charters Towers, in western Queensland.

Early in the 1880s the country's first cycling journal, *Bicycle*, was founded, but survived only a few months. It was followed by *Bicycling News*, which lasted about eighteen months. The third journal, *Australian Cycling News*, folded in 1889 after a sporadic existence.

Although a reported 1,500 high wheel bicycles were imported into New South Wales alone in 1887, they would never become the mount of the masses. By the end of the decade cycling was well established but the machines, being very expensive and difficult to ride, were essentially limited to a small segment of society.

In 1884 Alf Edward, on his high wheeler, became the first to cycle from Melbourne to Sydney, taking eight and a half days for the 931 kilometre (578 mile) trip along the Hume Highway. That same year another high wheel rider managed the 725 kilometre (450 mile) journey from Melbourne to Adelaide.

Australia's most famous high wheeler cyclist was George Burston, the son of Samuel Burston, a successful storekeeper in Flinders Street, Melbourne. George remained a director of Samuel Burston & Co Ltd until his death in 1924, and his financial stability enabled him to devote much time to cycling. He helped found the Melbourne Bicycle Club in 1878 and before the introduction of the pneumatic tyre held the Australian 100-mile (161 km) road record of 8 hours 9 minutes.

In November 1888 George Burston left Melbourne with H.R. Stokes on a round-the-world cycling trip. They travelled via Java, Singapore, Penang, Rangoon, India, Egypt, Palestine, Asia Minor, Sicily, Europe, the British Isles and the United States. They were the only Australians, and among the few world cyclists, to complete it on ordinary bicycles. His account of the trip was published in *The Australasian* and subsequently as *Round About the World on Bicycles* (Melbourne, 1890). He later made at least three more cycling journeys abroad. He took up the pneumatic-tyred safety bicycle with equal enthusiasm. In 1893 George helped form the League of Victorian

Wheelmen and long remained active in its administration. In 1894 Burston became the first to cycle across the Mount Hotham area of the Australian Alps, travelling from Omeo to Bright.

George Burston and H.R. Stokes

The Safety Bicycle

The safety bicycle changed everything. The machine's speed, safety, ease of riding and progressively decreasing cost resulted in it quickly capturing the imagination of Australians. It is impossible to determine exactly when the first safety bicycle (based on the diamond frame concept) reached Australia. The earliest specific reference is Joseph Pearson's importation of one into New South Wales in 1887, with accounts suggesting that they were commercially available in Melbourne in 1889. The pneumatic tyre, re-invented by Dunlop in 1888, was definitely fitted to commercial machines in Melbourne in 1890.

During the 1890s a cycling craze swept Australia and the country found itself in the mainstream of the world bicycle boom. Riding schools were established advertising imported cycle instructors. Doctors debated the effects of riding upon the human body and asked such questions as 'does cycling enlarge the hands and feet?'; one writer's reply was 'If only

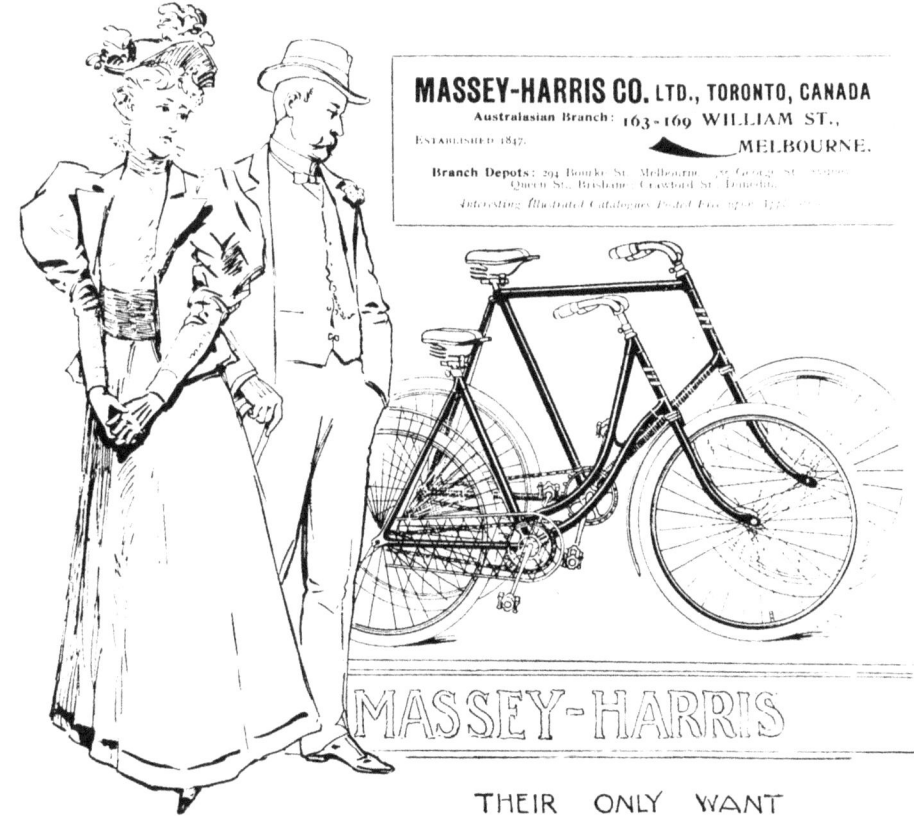

The Austral Wheel, January 1898

Mac Robertson's Royal Cycle Instructor
(PROFESSOR C. H. ECKENSTEIN).
INSTRUCTOR to THE PRINCESS OF WALES, DUKE AND DUCHESS OF CONNAUGHT, LORD LENNOX, LADY AND SIR EDWARD CLARKE, PRINCESS PLESS, LORD AND LADY BRASSEY, AND GOVERNMENT HOUSE PARTY.
CYCLING EVENTS TAUGHT:— Tent Pegging, Tilting the Ring, Polo, and Musical Cycle Quadrille, Plain and Fancy Riding.
Our Musical Cycle Hall: 217 to 230 Argyle Street, Fitzroy
FULL PARTICULARS ON APPLICATION. TELEPHONE 930.

The Austral Wheel, September 1896

some of the insane people who suggest such things would take to cycling themselves, and thus enlarge their brains, it would be better for everybody'. Arguments were mounted and countered as to which was the best food, drink and clothing for cyclists. The Melbourne 'Psycho' dealer announced the arrival of 'genuine Chicago chewing gum of various flavours', though some had doubts about the propriety of 'jaws and pedals going together'.

Some clergymen questioned the morality of Sunday cycling and to counter them scores of churchgoers were quickly organised to ride to church. Cyclistes, as female riders were then commonly known, took to the streets and roads, raising many questions about dress, morals and physical effects. Young girls were warned that bicycle seats could create 'heaps of troubles for their womanhood'. There was debate about the appropriate clothing (skirts versus bloomers) and whether some women should be riding at all. A U.S. judge's ruling that 'I will not allow a fallen woman to ride … promiscuously about the city and suburbs on a wheel … doing a great deal of harm not only to uncontaminated boys who ride wheels but innocent girls as well', was reprinted in Perth since it reflected a 'matter which at present is too painfully apparent in our own city'. And who would chaperone on those now-possible 100-miles-in-a-day trips (161 km) was no mean question.

Cycle racing became big business and gripped the public imagination to a degree almost incomprehensible today. In Melbourne crowds of 40,000

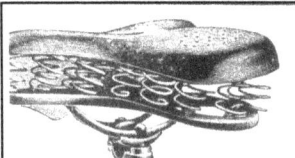

The Austral Wheel, May 1897

The Austral Wheel, January 1899

to 65,000 turned out for the two-day annual Austral Wheel and Australian Natives' Association cycle races. Prize money was lucrative, the riding hard, the riders harder, gambling heavy, and corruption rampant. Despite the fact that the sport was not a paragon of purity, the exciting racing kept the crowds coming. The intertwining of racing performance and cycle sales resulted in an uneasy alliance of manufacturers, sales agencies, riders, officials and hangers-on.

The publishing world saw the creation of many cycle magazines. Every colony had at least one; in New South Wales, Victoria and Western Australia several were simultaneously in print at one time or another during the decade. Virtually every newspaper and magazine had a cycling column and

The Austral Wheel, November 1898

an occasional editorial discussing the machine. The bicycle was advocated, lampooned, criticised, supported or denounced by various publishers and writers through cartoons, stories, poems and articles.

1893 – The Landmark Year

By 1893 use of the bicycle had begun to spread beyond the province of urban-based tourers to encompass the rural realm. Of great significance, the first overland ride—from the Gulf of Carpentaria in the far north, to Melbourne—conclusively demonstrated the machine's feasibility for outback use.

Percy Armstrong and R. Craig

Percy Armstrong and R. Craig left Croydon, Queensland in mid-August on heavy, cushion-tyred safeties bound for Sydney. From Croydon the two riders made for coastal Townsville, whence they headed more or less due south, meandering along stock routes through south central Queensland and northern New South Wales. The progress of the Croydon-Sydney journey was followed only sporadically in Australian newspapers because the pair spent much of their time away from towns. When they arrived in Sydney near the end of September, having covered nearly 2,000 miles (3,200 km), one journalist noted it as the first time the new machine had been 'advertised to some purpose'. Armstrong and Craig's ride had shown that the bicycle was capable of long-term use in rural areas, and the 50 miles (80 km) per day average on cushion-tyred machines and country roads and tracks was impressive.

Craig remained in Sydney but a local cycle agent offered Armstrong the use of a new bicycle with Dunlop pneumatic tyres with which to continue on to Melbourne. After a brief rest Armstrong set out and on his first two days covered 114 miles and 134 miles (184 km and 216 km), respectively, including night riding. Over the next couple of days heavy rain forced him to cross creeks on railway bridges, the muddy roads were badly cut up by teamsters, and he had to do a 'great amount of walking'. On his last night he ran into a culvert and tore out four spokes. After spending several hours by firelight respacing the remaining ones and a brief rest he remounted and arrived in Melbourne near mid day. Altogether he covered 578 miles (931 km) in 4 days 3¾ hours, averaging 138 miles (222 km) per day.

Armstrong's solo dash to Melbourne was closely followed in the newspapers and demonstrated the high rate of speed attainable on country roads using pneumatic tyres. Although Percy Armstrong was no ordinary cyclist, he had shown what the common rider could aspire to. In the process he had become the first to pedal across Australia.

2 Western Australia

Western Australia is huge, covering one-third of the Australian continent. In America, if you draw a line from the Canadian border to Mexico, through Denver, Western Australia is equivalent to everything west of that line. Most of the state is relatively flat with the exception of a small range of low mountains in the southwest, the rugged Kimberleys in the extreme northwest, and an occasional mountain range in between, where only a few peaks reach 3000 feet (900 m). A large portion is comprised of the Yilgarn Plateau, one of the oldest surfaces on earth and lying only a few hundred feet above sea level. Perth, the only city in the state, is in the southwest corner with a climate much like San Diego's, and the extreme north of the state experiences severe tropical monsoon rains in the summer. Most of the remainder is arid, large swathes of it covered by the Gibson Desert and aptly named Great Sandy Desert. And as for heat—the town of Marble Bar holds the world record of 100 °F (37.8 °C) or more for 160 consecutive days.

Unlike in the eastern colonies cycling was slow to develop in Western Australia. Perth had not been settled until 1829 and there were still only

some 50,000 people in the entire colony in 1891. In the days of the high wheelers the riders were few in number and significant cycling interest came about only with the gradual introduction of safety bicycles. Even then Perth cyclists did not venture far. The notoriously sandy roads around the town, considerable distances between the few scattered settlements, and inland heat inhibited cycle touring.

In September 1892 everything changed when gold was discovered at Coolgardie, some 350 miles (564 km) east of Perth. Over the next few years the various Westralian goldfields would become the scene of the world's largest gold rush, spread across a vast area the size of Arizona and half of Utah (or Denmark and Germany) combined. The first known inland use of a bicycle was a 200 mile (320 km) ride from Mullewa, a small settlement 300 miles (480 km) north of Perth, east to Cue, on the newly developing Murchison goldfield. Two months later two cyclists pedalled 450 miles (730 km) roundtrip from Perth to Southern Cross (over half way to Coolgardie), the furthermost eastern town at the time. It was 'the longest and most difficult ride yet attempted in the colony' and a portent of things to come.

Many early travellers walked to the eastern goldfield from Southern Cross, often throwing their swags on accompanying teamsters' wagons to ease the burden. Coaches were available, but were expensive, crowded and

Cyclists celebrating the completion of the railway line to Coolgardie in 1896

uncomfortable, and often meant as much getting out and walking as riding along the sandy track. Some travellers eventually used bicycles, although it is not known who took the first machine past Southern Cross, or when. The first definite reference is in 1893, by which time cyclists were already employed in delivering messages between Southern Cross and Coolgardie. However, given the popularity of the machine in the eastern colonies, the large number of Victorians involved in the rush, and the publicising of rapid rides between Perth and Southern Cross, the bicycle was undoubtedly introduced to the eastern goldfields very early.

A number of conditions on the newly opening goldfields were conducive to the adoption of the bicycle. In the summer Kalgoorlie temperatures range up to 46 °C (115 °F). Rainfall averages only 265 mm (10.43 inches) annually and decreases to the north and east. Even worse for the early prospectors, 1890–1903 was a period of marked deficiency of rainfall on the fields and during the years 1892–94 the area was subjected to a particularly severe drought. In such circumstances the scarcity of water and stock feed and their high cost made the upkeep of camels and horses a burden and often impossible. This is reflected in the columns of the early newspapers which are full of comments about the number of dead and dying horses, often in the main streets. Riding and pack camels, imported to fill the gap, cost several times as much as a bicycle.

The Westralian Niche

In those circumstances the bicycle played a role unlike anywhere else in the world. In December 1894 Kalgoorlie's *Western Argus* editorialised in its third issue that 'One of the great institutions in the district is the trusty bicycle, a machine which is daily becoming more useful. There are a good many machines in Hannan's, White Feather, Coolgardie and surrounding districts, and it is no uncommon sight to see ministers of religion, business people & c. making their way on the iron steed to Kurnalpi and other districts'. One writer estimated that Coolgardie 'had more bicycles in proportion to population than any other Australian town. Looking down Bayley Street the first thing noticed by a stranger is the great number of cycles lining both sides of the street, and dodging hither and thither the whole length of this well-known thoroughfare, giving it a very modern aspect'.

The Story of Australian Cycling

The reaction was echoed by many visitors to the fields. After arriving in Coolgardie at night Henry Walker's first impression upon awakening the next morning was that 'bustling merchants and clerks were hurrying past on bicycles to their various occupations'. Julius Price noted the town's 'dusty roadway crowded with teams, camel caravans, buggies, horsemen, and bicycles' and his hand sketch of Coolgardie's main street featured a cyclist in the forefront. A lady described Coolgardie's streets as the 'most level and the best for cycling I have ever ridden on'. The bustle was not restricted to Coolgardie. A visitor to Cue, 400 miles (645 km) northwest, commented that 'The first thing that struck [me] ... was the number of bicycles in use ... everyone seemed in too much of a hurry to walk'.

And it wasn't just in and around the towns. Many visitors commented upon the bicycle's use both for rushing strikes and for general prospecting throughout the Yilgarn Plateau. At a deep lead discovery at Kanowna in late 1897 the roads were described by one newspaper as crowded with 'cyclists, buggies, etc.'. In referring to one man's pegging out a claim in late 1898 the

A crowd gathered in Kalgoorlie to hear Father Long announce the location of a gold find. Although a hoax, a rush followed, including numerous cyclists hoping to beat others to the strike

Coolgardie Miner commented that 'almost as soon as he had put his pegs in, he was surrounded by the usual crowd of peggars on bike, buggy, cart and shanks' pony'. In Kalgoorlie in 1895, when Father Long announced the site where the 'Sacred Nugget' had supposedly been found (it was a hoax), the crowd of intending rushers included many cyclists. A stampede followed his announcement with 'horses galloping, cyclists scorching, and buggies madly driving'.

A famous incident involving the bicycle's use was a rumoured find

Studio photograph of a prospector on his return from the Mt Ragged gold rush

of gold at Mount Ragged, located some 240 miles (385 km) southeast of Coolgardie, near Israelite Bay. Through isolated and harsh country several men pushed their machines through thick vegetation that had to be occasionally cut to allow passage. The report proved groundless and some of the cyclists, arriving early on the scene, turned back many men while returning to Coolgardie. The episode was widely reported in eastern newspapers and one writer noted that one man's 'appearance was most pitiable and bore eloquent testimony to the hardship he had gone through; though strangely enough, his bicycle was comparatively uninjured'.

There was hardly an activity on the fields that seemingly could not benefit from the bicycle. *The Sydney Mail*'s mining column was normally devoted to such matters as the depths of shafts and assay reports. However, from the Western Australian correspondent there were occasional discussions of mine managers and visitors from the east using the bicycle during their surveys of facilities. One pedalled 520 miles (835 km) on a tour of mining activities between Kalgoorlie and Mount Magnet. A government employee serving plaints out of Broad Arrow received 1 shilling per mile and 5 shillings per plaint served. He originally carried out his task on horseback and with camels but switched when he found 'the bicycle being far and away the best for travelling purposes' in the area.

Given the machine's ubiquitous use, bicycle paths quickly appeared throughout the goldfields along with accompanying signboards, since directions and distances were critical and a wrong turn could prove dangerous. Cycle paths—acknowledged as such—often were no more than the informal

The Rev. Thomas Trestrail, Methodist minister who served the Coolgardie parish, circa 1894-5. He was among the first Australian clergyman to use the bicycle extensively

marking of a frequented route. On the other hand a contract was specifically let for the cutting of a cycle path between Mulline and Menzies in 1898 and grants for other cycle paths were sporadically promised to district roads boards, though many remained promises. The Yalgoo Roads Board imposed an annual cycle tax but it met strenuous opposition as cyclists felt, and probably rightly, that the taxes would not be applied to cycle path construction but would be lost in general revenue.

The Cycling Telegraph

The rapid growth of Western Australia following the Coolgardie find of late 1892 created, among other things, extensive and voluminous communications requirements. These posed enormous problems and provided the basis for the first important use of the bicycle in rural Australia. The colony's population tripled to over 160,000 by 1897 and nearly half of the men in Western Australia were scattered about the eastern fields. Ultimately most of the gold was found not in alluvial material but in reefs and companies had to be set up to handle the large operations required to extract it. In 1894 alone some sixty companies were formed to invest in gold mining; by the end of 1896 there were over three hundred. The large population and heavy investment combined with government activities resulted in a great need for communications as residents corresponded with friends and relatives elsewhere; the press maintained a continuous stream of words chronicling the fortunes of the fields; and the very existence of mining companies, prospectors and brokers depended upon information exchange.

The most severe communications problems were faced from mid-1893 through 1896. As prospectors explored throughout the interior, the posting of a claim or the rumour of a find was sufficient to cause several hundred men to immediately set off. Some of the rumours were completely groundless and some finds were disappointing and relatively few prospectors remained. A few were initially fabulous, such as the Londonderry rush south of Coolgardie, but did not live up to expectation. Others such as at Menzies and Kalgoorlie, proved rich and the populations progressively grew. The growth and continual redistribution of the population, coupled with the ephemeral nature of many of the communities, made it hard to rationally allocate postal and telegraphic staff and facilities.

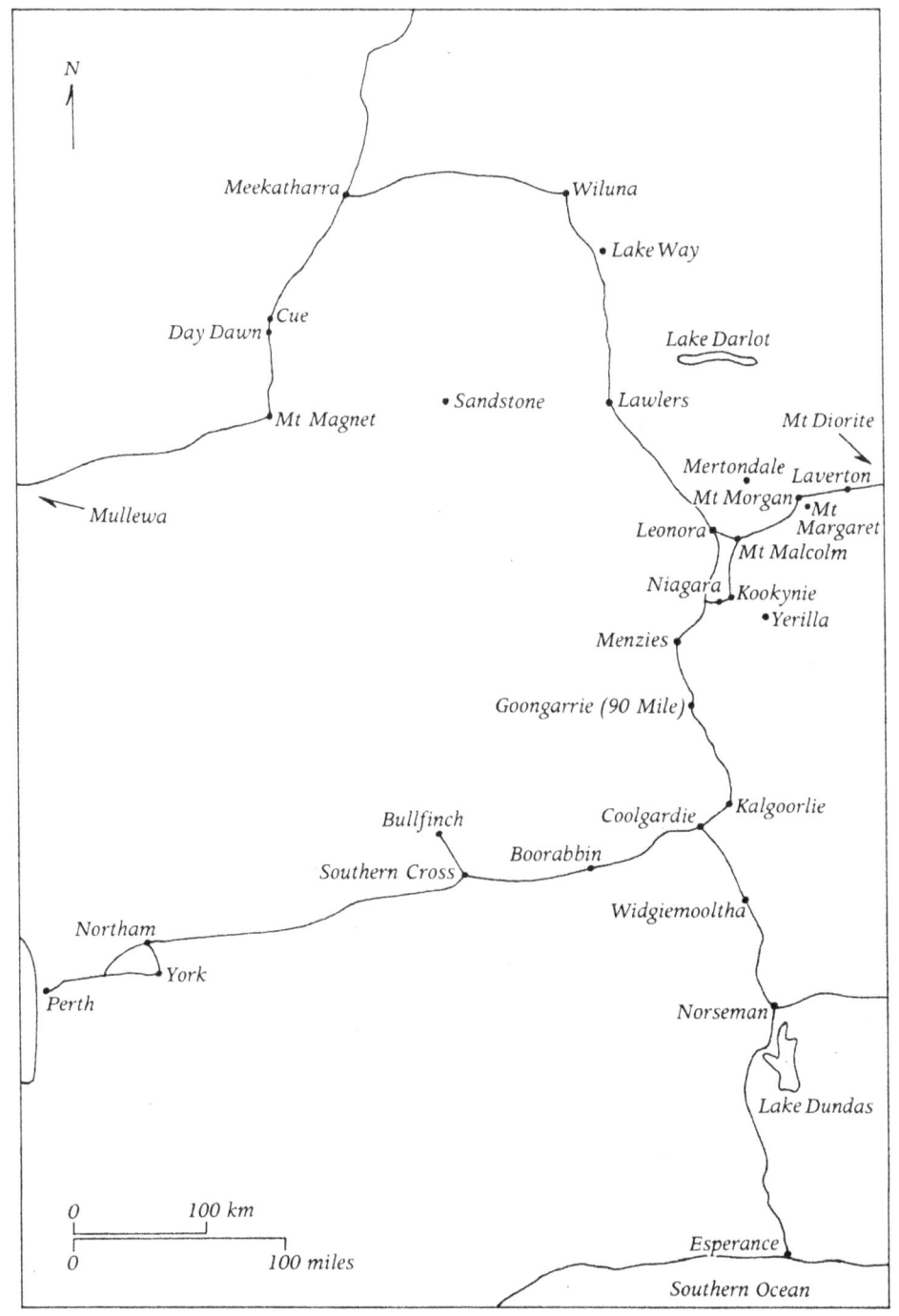

The principal communities of the eastern and Murchison goldfields of Western Australia circa 1900. The region was laced by an extensive formal and ad hoc network of roads, bush tracks, and camel and bicycle pads

The first official Coolgardie post office was not opened until September 1893, one year after the initial find. While later mining centres generally acquired post offices more quickly, the delays were often long. To provide services in the interim the post office frequently paid private individuals,

The busineess card of the Koolgardie Cycle Express Co., probably printed in late 1895. It was one of several such firms operating on the Western Australian goldfields in the mid-1890s

known as Receivers of Mail Bags (R.M.B.), to handle mail in a particular location. Most communities, however, experienced a lag between initial settlement and institution even of R.M.B. services. Kalgoorlie (originally called Hannans) was rushed in June 1893 but did not have a post office until eight months later, despite an extremely large population around the immediate area. Menzies, founded in late 1894, obtained its R.M.B. only in March 1895 and a permanent post office seven months after that. The Dundas field was proclaimed in August 1893 but no post office established for twenty months. It was not until late 1895 that the demand for formal postal facilities in most centres had been satisfied.

The establishment of official facilities did not in itself guarantee reliable, fast communication. The task of the R.M.B.s was 'indifferently performed on many occasions' and delivery was often frustratingly slow. The Telegraph Department in particular was unable to cope. Services were chaotic and messages paid for at telegraphic rates were at times sent to Perth by ordinary mail. The editor of the *Coolgardie Review*, referring to the situation in late 1895, was not concerned about the delays: 'Folks say that they can get their telegrams through by team almost as rapidly as by wire, and that they can place more reliance upon a camel than upon the telegraph wires. Well, what if they can. Surely it does not make much difference to a business man if his wires happen to be delayed a week or ten days'.

Very few others shared his view. The system was so overwhelmed by the end of 1895 that communications were a subject of large protests held in Coolgardie and Kalgoorlie. Amidst this erratic, uncertain and obviously unsatisfactory situation several bicycle delivery services were started, though it is not clear who was the first. They ranged from major networks to individual riders taking casual orders.

After completing his overland ride in September 1893 Percy Armstrong went to Western Australia, arriving on the goldfields in March 1894. He established a Special Bicycle Express service sometime thereafter, locating his office near the Coolgardie Post Office. Later in the year he also founded the first bicycle sales agency on the field, which eventually expanded to become the largest and most extensive network in the colony, with outlets in nearly all goldfields communities, Perth and Fremantle. Armstrong's cycle delivery network served the entire eastern goldfield and extended across to Cue on the Murchison field as well, with as many as ten riders working for him. One writer, after examining the company's books, concluded that Armstrong's riders covered a total of 260,000 miles (420,000 km) during the network's existence.

The Coolgardie Cycle Express Co. initially delivered between Coolgardie and Southern Cross but the network quickly expanded. By early 1894 it was serving not only outlying communities but was extended 140 miles (225 km) south to Dundas and Norseman. The following year it included Menzies and as far north as Lake Darlot. Regular services were scheduled to these centres in addition to the 'special' messages that could be contracted at any time; the company's business card listed at least six riders in service. There were numerous other scheduled and 'special' cycle messenger services on the goldfields. Many cycle dealers carried messages 'to all outlying districts' when requested, while some services pedalled mail, newspapers and parcels on specific regularly scheduled routes.

The forte of the cycle messengers was rapid delivery throughout an immense area. The straight line distance from the most southerly to most northerly communities was some 700 kilometres (435 miles), e.g. San Diego to San Francisco (Paris to Monaco), and from east to west some 600 kilometres (370 miles), e.g. Phoenix to Los Angeles (Paris nearly to Munich). David Carnegie noted that the cyclists could do 100 miles (161 km) in a day and W.B. Kimberley wrote that when 'messages had to be hurriedly delivered ... a cyclist was approached in preference to camel or horseman'. The speed and endurance of the cycle riders was marvelled at in the circumstances. The 190-kilometre (118 mile) ride over the notoriously sandy route from Coolgardie to Southern-Cross (the inland terminus of the telegraph line for some time) was done in twelve hours, in contrast to the record camel ride of 21 hours.

Armstrong's first ride was an 85-mile (137 km) delivery, returning the following day. On one occasion, he rode 105 miles (169 km) from Menzies to Coolgardie in thirteen hours and continued on to Widgiemooltha the same night—a total of 152 miles (224 km) in nineteen hours. In the next two days he rode an additional 190 miles (306 km), averaging 114 miles (183 km) per day over three days; this compares favourably with his 138 miles (222 km) per day between Sydney and Melbourne. Because riders were able to cover the 25 miles (40 km) between Kalgoorlie and Coolgardie in less than 1½ hours, they were hired to make urgent runs between the two when delays occurred in telegraph transmission. In 1897 a pair of riders delivered a dispatch for a mining company between Cue and Lake Darlot in 61 hours. The ride had been done quicker but the fact that the riders turned around and completed a 540-mile (870 km) return trip in 136 hours in continuous 'rain, adverse roads, and mud' made it newsworthy.

Such efforts contributed to an almost legendary status for the special riders who received great respect on the goldfields for maintaining a quick link with the rest of the world. They carried as much mail as possible and thus little in the way of 'blankets or provisions except of the scantiest description, and took their chance of hitting off the camp of some wayfarer'. When a cyclist was caught between towns at night, an individual along the road 'would always be ready to show what hospitality he could, to messengers of so much importance. To have to part with one of your blankets on a cold night for the benefit of another traveller, is one of the severest exercises of self-denial'. A handwritten message carried by a special cyclist from one client put it more succinctly: 'Let him have anything he may want for the road and oblige'. Failing that, they had 'perforce to make the best of a fire as a substitute for a blanket, and to be content with a hungry stomach, in place of having a meal'.

Such services were not cheap. One newspaper reported that some 'very large sums have been paid' on occasion. The first riders between Southern Cross and Coolgardie reportedly charged as much as £25 per message, which was the cost of steerage class passage from London to Fremantle in 1894. With the establishment of regular services and competition the charges decreased. Prices depended upon distance, urgency and weight, but the Coolgardie Cycle Express Co. applied standard rates for letters with normal postal and telegraphic costs added to the cycle charges, where appropriate. Some routes were partially subsidised by mining companies to assure regular service in their district. For the messenger companies it appears to have been a lucrative business.

The major cycle messenger services were closed down in late 1896 or early 1897 as telegraph lines and regular mail services were established. But given the close association of cycle messengers with cycle agencies, the closure of the messenger services did not mean the end of cycle deliveries. Special cyclists continued operating where they were quicker, the regular services were too infrequent, the government could not cope with the demand, and in isolated areas. As late as 1898 Express Delivery Cycles in Coolgardie was delivering messages, newspapers or parcels at short notice to 'all parts of the Fields'. Elderly goldfield residents recalled that isolated mining operations continued to use occasional cycle messengers up to about 1920.

The cycle messenger riders demonstrated the great practical value of the machine to a local and national audience and the Western Australian Commissioner of Lands lauded the riders for playing an integral role in the development of the goldfields. It is impossible to quantify their contribution, as it will never be known what fortunes were won or lost by the cycle riders' deliveries. As with all information conveyance, the cost of transmission is often no reflection of the value of what is conveyed.

Camel Pads

There is nothing more fascinating about the use of bicycles in rural Australia than the relationship between cyclists and camels. As Herbert Barker wrote, 'scores of Western Australian gold towns depended on the Afghans' pack camels for all but heavy mining machinery and building materials. The strings of pack camels formed smooth tracks which delighted people on bicycles … They spoke very highly of camel pads for bicycle tracks and I can quite believe it. On stony country, pack camels in single file very soon … swept loose stones away, or if the ground was damp and the camels were

Goldfields travellers

heavily loaded their broad feet pressed the stones into the soil. On sandy country their feet tamped the sand, making it firm enough for a bicycle'. Jack Costello, a Kalgoorlie reporter who still cycled around the district in the 1930s, found that the passage of a single string of only twelve camels notably improved a riding surface. Where broad wagon tyres had been used in conjunction with camels the resultant tracks, even on hard, stony roads, were often 'so smooth that you could walk barefooted along them' and remained firm even when covered with water.

Riders extolled the virtues of the camel pads and went out of their way to use them. A Coolgardie resident stated that 'nothing in life here can surpass a spin along one of our good camel pads'. Another described them as 'a wheelman's riding luxury'. Shearers along the Strzelecki Track made use of them, and in New South Wales Albert Ford found it 'a pleasure to get on these camel team tracks'. The quality of the pads is illustrated by the results of a road race at Mount Magnet, Western Australia in September

1899. Using camel pads a rider broke both the 25- and 40-mile (40 and 64 km) Australasian unpaced road records. First reports of the race were not believed in Perth, and the *W.A. Cyclist* commented that 'personally we think there is a mistake somewhere'. However, after checking further the journal aided in the formal submission of the record claim.

Because the pad was so smooth, subsequent camel drivers and cyclists tended to use the same narrow path, and unlike other roads and tracks, camel pads frequently resembled narrow alleys through the bush. Early camel tracks (and other routes as well) were often circuitous, because the first person to pass through was not clear as to exact directions, or deviated from one water source to another and subsequent travellers tended to follow the original tracks. Eventually travellers took shortcuts and improvements were made by surveyors. One cyclist observed that 'the best pads run along the telegraph lines, thus being the shortest as well as the best routes'.

For cyclists, the benefits derived from the camels were unquestionable though camels were reportedly disturbed by cyclists. Near Yardea Station, South Australia the James brothers reported that a string of camels stampeded at the sight of the machines and riders even though they were pedalling slowly. A Western Australian rider noted that the 'usually stolid and indifferent beasts' were frightened of bicycles. When approached from behind the camels would rush about, snap lines, and create chaos generally'.

As late as the 1930s there were still a few cycle pads in use about the Western Australian goldfields with some still having boards and sleepers over small watercourses. By the mid-1970s a few routes could still be detected about Coolgardie, between Bulong and Kalgoorlie, and near some of the old mining settlements in the Murchison area. Before long, however, plant growth and wind and water erosion will have erased all vestiges of the most extensive cycle path network in the world in the 1890s and the largest yet seen in Australia.

The Goldfields Bicycle Pad Protection League

The importance of, and problems associated with, goldfields cyclists' pads led to the formation of the Goldfields Bicycle Pad Protection League, unquestionably one of the more unusual bicycle action groups ever seen—if not in its objectives, at least in its circumstances. It had its origins in a letter written by C.H.A. Stone, secretary of the Broad Arrow Cyclists' Association (Broad Arrow was a small community 24 miles (37 km) north of Kalgoorlie), and published in the *Broad Arrow Standard* on 30 June 1897:

> ... What cyclist has not bitterly felt cruel and unjust destruction of our pads, and longed for the time when they should be protected from general traffic. Who can deny that our pad from Broad Arrow to Kalgoorlie was made by ourselves, is in nobody's way, yet has been cruelly cut up from end to end. All the shorter ones have suffered likewise; ... we are a large and powerful body, embracing all classes, from the miner who rides to work, to the parson who rides to church ... we have come to look on our bicycles as indispensable ... considering that we make our own pads, it is only just and right that we should have the exclusive right of them ... almost every existing track is on the site of one of our pads ... A new pad is made; a horseman comes along (most likely a mounted trooper), sees the pad going in his direction, and follows it, leaving large hoof marks for us to bump over. Along comes the baker, the butcher, and mining expert likewise, and the track is then ready for the water cart or heavy team; our pad, of course, disappears; we make a fresh one, and along comes the procession again. I notice that Kanowna cyclists have decided to form a new pad to Kalgoorlie, logging it in various places to stop the general traffic, and they propose to post printed notices along it asking horsemen to keep off it. To my mind the logging may to some extent keep buggies off, but the posting of notices seems to me like filling the manger with good hay and posting a notice asking the steed to eat his straw bed ... I think, for a start, we might get a bill introduced into Parliament, reserving a strip of, say, three yards on each side of all telegraph lines outside Coolgardie for cyclists alone, and making it punishable by heavy penalty for any horseman or driver of horses found within that area (except of course crossing it) ... the trouble I write of has rankled in our bosoms quite long enough. A monster petition to Parliament, or even perhaps to the Government, backed up by the various Road Boards, and certainly backed up by the League of West Australian Wheelmen, might be successful. Concerted action is necessary ...

Stone's grievance quickly reached F.C.B. Vosper, the local Member of the Legislative Assembly of Western Australia. In reply Vosper promised to bring the question forward in Parliament if properly briefed, but that first a 'unified expression of opinion should be obtained from the cyclists of the fields'. The *West Australian Wheelman*, published in Perth, printed Stone's letter in mid-July. The *Kalgoorlie Miner* pointed out that cycling on

This bicycle pad southeast of Kalgoorlie was photographed in the early 1930s by Jack Costello, a local reporter. This was one remnant of a system dating from the 1890s that represented the most extensive bicycle path network yet seen in Australia

the fields was 'the principal means of inter-communication between centres where the railway has not penetrated. As a matter of fact, on the fields it has come to be regarded as essential, and of course under the conditions just mentioned it forms the one and only mode of rapid transit ... the army of cyclists in respect of their numbers, if nothing else, should command respect when they give utterance to grievance, suggestion or request'.

Four days later the Perth *Morning Herald* suggested that if the matter reached Parliament 'it is likely that their request for protection and encouragement will be favorably considered'. It also indicated that goldfields cyclists would receive cooperation and support from cyclists in other parts of the colony. Goldfields clergymen, many of whom relied on the cycle for

Cyclists were common elements of many Western Australian newspaper photographs in the 1890s

travel, supported the movement and Percy Armstrong noted widespread enthusiasm for it during his August tour of the goldfields. Buoyed by the support and publicity, a meeting was held in Broad Arrow, a petition initiated, and names collected from nearby communities and the Murchison district. Stone felt 'confident that we only have to ask Government or Parliament for protection of our just rights and we shall receive it'.

But not one goldfields bicycle club or its parent organisation took up the issue publicly. A survey of various cycle club meetings indicated that they were only interested in obtaining cycle racing facilities and assigning racing dates; the broader interests of the cycling contingent were of no apparent concern. Moreover, there was hostility between the goldfields cycling organisation and the metropolitan-based League of Wheelmen. This resulted partly from jealousy, because the goldfields races were better known across Australia, had larger attendances, and were more remunerative than the Perth ones. But even had the two organisations been on friendly terms, the League of Wheelmen also had no interest in such non-racing matters as better roads (they were criticised about this for years, but to no avail). The unfortunate result for the Bicycle Pad Protection League was a complete lack of assistance or support from any cycling organisation or formal bicycle club in the colony—the kind of 'united expression of opinion' Vospers probably had in mind.

Though the petition was forwarded to Vosper by late August he had not vented the matter in Parliament by mid-December and Parliamentary records do not indicate that he ever did. Aside from a brief note in the *Broad Arrow Standard* in December, no publication—not even the specialised bicycle journals—ever again mentioned the movement or the fate of the petition. The treatment accorded the petition, however, was hinted at obliquely by the *Broad Arrow Standard* in a brief, somewhat bitter news item on 20 November, noting the visit of Mr and Mrs Vosper to nearby Bulong and Kanowna, but not Broad Arrow: 'unless Mr Vosper had very strong reasons to stop him coming this way he slurred us ... As a matter of fact we have a strong suspicion of the why and wherefore that Mr Vosper temporarily gave Broad Arrow the cold shoulder'. As is often the case in political matters, the full story of the Goldfields Bicycle Pad Protection League will probably never be known. Nonetheless, the cyclists' right to the exclusive use of the tracks and pads they had established and maintained was recognised and honoured by many horsemen and teamsters.

3 Maps, Guides and English

The pneumatic-tyred safety bicycle opened up mass tourism in Australia. With men and women able to readily pedal 100 kilometres (62 miles) a day and more, relatively long weekend and holiday trips were feasible, unconfined to railway, riverboat or coaching routes. An immediate result was that many found themselves lost on country roads—until then the province of local residents, coachmen, teamsters, and commercial travellers who knew where they were going—with few signs indicating which road led where, or how far it was to the next community. There was little information available as to road conditions, which were highly variable from area to area, season to season, and hour to hour, depending upon the weather, and few indications of the location and quality of eating and sleeping facilities.

Jenolan Caves, New South Wales, 1900

The early riders quickly built up a store of information and by 1898 individuals had produced numerous road maps and groups such as The New South Wales Cyclists' Touring Union were established. These groups enrolled members, contracted for local representatives in country towns to assist tourists passing through, negotiated discounts at hotels for club members, provided maps and guides, offered tips on touring and advised on the care of bicycles. This allayed many doubts and the cumulative effect was a new national consciousness with respect to tourism in Australia. In the process cyclists established the basic principles upon which later motoring organisations were founded and provided the impetus for the establishment of state tourist bureaus.

Road Maps and Guides

The modern Australian road map—designed specifically to inform travellers of road surface conditions, distances, directions and facilities en route—was developed by and for cycle tourists during the 1890s. Prior to that time there were very few maps available and none with the details cyclists required. The scale was often too small, minor roads sometimes ignored, gazetted roads marked which did not yet exist, some very good roads not marked at all, and surfaces rarely described.

By the mid-1890s the continent's first mass consumption road maps were produced. Some were crude. Saxton's and Buckle's *1895 Cyclists' and Tourists' Handbook of Victoria: Showing Upwards of 10,000 Miles of Roads* did just that, but little more. It had no direction arrow, scale, or key and gave no indication of hills, slopes or road surfaces. The distances between towns were not marked on the map itself, but included in a separate 72-page booklet.

The major developments came in 1896 through the efforts of George Broadbent and Major M. O'Farrell in Victoria, and Joseph Pearson in New South Wales, individuals who, during the course of their extensive cycle journeys, had compiled a huge amount of information on touring and road conditions.

Joseph Pearson produced the first New South Wales road map in 1896, a copy of which appeared in the *Review of Reviews* in July. Influenced by the quality and availability of maps he had seen during a cycling trip in England

Joseph Pearson, 1900, a few days after his bicycle ascent of Mt Kosciusko

in 1893, he progressively improved and revised his own over the years as well as producing a series of touring guides for cyclists and motorists, published by H.E.C. Robinson.

'Genial Joe' was one of the original members of the New South Wales cycling community, reportedly riding the first penny-farthing in the colony. In 1882 he took up cycling on a regular basis and competed in road races on solid-tyred high wheelers. He eventually gave away competition and engaged in long tours during which he kept detailed records of road conditions and distances. He was influential in cycling matters in the colony, served on the Executive Board of the Cyclist's Touring Union, was a member of numerous bicycle clubs, and later served as adviser to the state government when the Tourist Bureau was being formed. During his 41 years of cycling he estimated that he rode about 180,000 miles (290,000 km), including reaching the top of Mt Kosciusko, Australia's highest peak, and could readily manage 100 miles per day on tours, even in hilly country, much to the awe (and consternation) of other riders. He financed his activities through a clothing store he operated in the King Street Arcade ('the finest display of gentlemen's mercery in the city, at popular prices'). In 1925 he wrote a booklet entitled *Reminiscences Including Cycling Experiences*, which was republished in 1933.

Pearson was particularly instrumental in helping the New South Wales Cyclists' Touring Union produce the *Cyclists' Handbook and Guide to the Roads of New South Wales* in 1898, the most comprehensive and detailed map and touring guide in Australia. It consisted of two small volumes held in a bound, pocket-sized case. The *Handbook*'s 136 pages provided information on gearing; care and repair of the machine; legal and medical tips; phases of the moon, and sun and moon rising and setting times; telegraphic, railway and steamer rates; the names of the local Touring Union Consuls (thirty-three of them, including such distant towns as Bourke and Bingara); and the Union's constitution, rules and member clubs. In addition the Union arranged for its members to receive discounts of 20 to 33⅓ per cent at many hotels, and listed the tariffs for 171 hotels throughout the state.

The 234-page *Guide* (including a folded map of the state) indicated intermediate and cumulative mileages between important towns; the formation of main and branch roads; dangerous gradients; where pushing was required; what the roads were like in varying weather conditions; the specific soil ('red clays', 'black soil'); where to cross rivers, depending upon the amount of water flowing at the time; and facts important to particular areas ('look out for bullocks')—all of this for several thousand miles of road.

In Victoria Major M. O'Farrell published the *Austral Wheel* from 1896 to 1900. It and the *Australian Cyclist* were the closest the colonies had to national cycling

A cyclist in the Goulburn River Valley, touring the Victorian Alps in 1908

journals but the *Austral Wheel* was far and away the best in coverage and quality, and widely plagiarised. Beginning in 1896 O'Farrell published a series of detailed maps in various issues. These maps described the roads, local vegetation and touring facilities en route, gave distances, and indicated

On the road to Merrijig, Victoria

hills and slopes by hachuring. In addition, they had a scale and direction arrow and classed roads as good, fair, or bad. The journal apparently printed not only the first road maps for some parts of Victoria, but for southeastern South Australia and parts of Tasmania as well. However, O'Farrell's maps were only included in the journal and were not available for separate public sale.

In 1896 George Broadbent also produced his first road map of Victoria, based upon many years of riding about the colony. A cycling racer and enthusiast, he set many Victorian and Australian road records both on high wheelers and safeties and was lauded in his day by the *Australian Cyclist* as 'the finest road rider that Australia has ever produced'. Broadbent, along with George Burston, was a founder of the League of Victorian Wheelmen in 1893. He went on to become a major influence in Victorian road and motoring activities, including being a founding member of the Royal Automobile Club of Victoria in 1903.

George Broadbent

Broadbent's maps indicated distances, general topography, and riding conditions—'good', 'fair' or 'ridden with difficulty'. In contrast to O'Farrell's maps in the *Austral Wheel*, Broadbent's maps were available for public sale. They were so popular that by 1898 a fourth edition was printed on linen. With continual revision and astute business practice Broadbent's maps became the state standard and the company was active for many decades.

In 1896 C.A.A. Schwaebsch published *The Cyclists' and Victorian Tourists' Road Guide, Part I—Eastern District* (there is no evidence that any were published for other parts of Victoria). The booklet contained ten maps printed in two colours and perforated for tearing out. One was of the Melbourne area within a radius of 10 miles (16 km) from the General Post Office, and others covered various districts as far east as Orbost. The booklet described road conditions and touring matters of interest and on the backs of the maps were listed cumulative mileages from Melbourne to the various communities.

Outside New South Wales and Victoria there were few similar maps produced. In South Australia in 1897 the *Adelaide Register* published one indicating roads within a 25-mile (40 km) radius of the GPO. It was reprinted as a pamphlet later in the year and issued in 1900 as an expanded touring guide. In 1898 the *South Australian Cyclist* produced what was possibly the first road map from Adelaide to Port Augusta.

It is not known how many copies of early road maps were produced. However, given that Broadbent sold some 110,000 in Victoria by 1910, and assuming that Joseph Pearson and H.E.C. Robinson were similarly prolific in New South Wales, probably well over 200,000 road maps were printed for separate sale in Australia by 1910, at which time there were only about 5,000 motor vehicles in the country.

The Australian Alps

During the late 1890s bicycle tourists pedalled or pushed over most of the major roads of the eastern highlands and into the Australian Alps. By mid-1898 their endeavours resulted in detailed alpine touring guides which allayed many doubts about such trips, made planning straightforward, and provided a great source of armchair reading for the many who would only travel there vicariously. The cumulative effect was an increasing awareness of Australia's mountains. As in so many ways in rural Australia, the human-engined device had opened up new opportunities and vistas.

Keep in mind that this was not modern mountain biking with sprung frames, umpteen gears and disc brakes. The machines at that time were fixed wheel, with a single gear, and many had no auxiliary brakes. They relied on back-pedalling—resisting the forward motion of the fixed wheel pedals—for stopping. This system was very tiring, dangerous and often inadequate during steep descents.

By 1894 riders were penetrating the fringes of the Australian Alps, which were within a day's journey from Melbourne. That year George Burston, who had graduated from high wheelers to safeties, became the first to cycle across the Mt Hotham area, travelling northwest from Omeo to Bright. In 1896 J. Railton became the second to pedal to Mt Hotham. Encountering

Touring cyclists in New South Wales, 1900

a heat wave of up to 105 °F (40.5 °C) in Harrietville, he rode some of the journey at night. Many roads were badly cut up by bullock teams. At one stage he was forced to walk down one very steep, rough eighteen-mile stretch, and had to get off and push his machine up numerous ascents. After 'doing this for miles uphill, one soon has enough of it'. Nonetheless he completed the 191 miles in eight days.

In December 1897 the *Austral Wheel Guide to the Victorian Alps* was published in Melbourne as a special supplement to the *Austral Wheel's* regular December issue. It contained photographs and descriptions of various Victorian alpine communities and touring routes, indicated road conditions, listed accommodation and eating facilities, and included numerous advertisements for hotels and guest houses. While nothing similar was produced for New South Wales, the detailed information in the New South Wales Cyclists' Touring Union's *Guide* of 1898—listing local Union representatives, train schedules and fares, hotel discounts for CTU

Wheeling Matilda

A roadside spring in the Victorian Alps, 1908

members, and road conditions—was far more useful in some respects than was the *Austral Wheel*'s guide.

In December 1898 W.R. Gainford and Eric Barling set out from Sydney to make the first bicycle ascent of Mt Kosciusko, taking the train as far as Goulburn. They pedalled to Jindabyne where a new 'Tourist Hotel' had recently opened. The rate for the trip to the summit of Mt Kosciusko was £1 per day per person for the provision of riding and pack horses, a tent, food and a guide's services. The first guide Gainford approached refused when told the bicycle was to go along. However, another agreed to conduct them to Kosciusko although he had reservations about whether the bicycle could be got up the mountain and as a precaution provided a second riding horse. As Barling's cycle frame had cracked during the ride from Goulburn to Jindabyne he rode a horse to the peak. During the 2½-day round trip from Jindabyne they coved an estimated sixty miles. Gainford rode horseback for five miles (8 km), managed to bicycle for twenty-five miles (40 km), and walked and pushed the machine for thirty miles (48 km). Gainford's description of the vistas and the camping spots they used suggest that the journey to Mt Kosciusko was not along the valley floor and over Charlotte Pass, but much higher, near the ridge of the Rams Head Range. When they reached the peak on 28 December they were greeted by two residents of the meteorological observatory who, cyclists themselves, 'enjoyed the novelty of cycling on the snowy track'. Gainford demonstrated that the trip could be accomplished by

Between Mansfield and Warburton, the Victorian Alps, early 1900s

a cyclist and garnered the laurel as the first to ride on the roof of Australia.

Joseph Pearson claimed, however, to have made the first 'true' ascent of the peak on a bicycle, in 1900, as he did not resort to the use of a horse at any time. Pearson's Kosciusko climb was only a small part of a ride from Sydney via Yass, Gundagai, Tumut, Kiandra, Adelong and Jindabyne, returning via Dalgety, Cooma and Bega. Another party was also touring the Kiandra area at the same time. This group carried an aneroid barometer and subsequently published a series of elevational profiles of most of the route in the *New South Wales Cycling Gazette*. They felt that the most suitable route to the summit was south from Kiandra, as the gradient was much more gradual than from Jindabyne. They also felt that 'a bicycle track could easily be constructed' along the existing track, the principal problem being tussock grass.

It is impossible to assess the extent of early alpine cycle touring. Though the *New South Wales Cycling Gazette* and Victorian journals cited various journeys to the southern tablelands and alpine areas in 'club notes', they tended to reflect the activities of local metropolitan club members. As only a small fraction of bicycle owners belonged to such clubs, many rides would have gone unreported.

The Bicycle and Australian English

By the mid-1890s many newspapers and magazines had instituted regular cycling columns. Cycle journals were imported (mostly from England and the United States), and several local ones were founded. The result for Australian English was the rapid infusion of a variety of words and phrases from overseas, along with some homegrown creations and adaptations. The following discussion is based upon research of written materials, as well as personal interviews carried out in the 1970s with Australians who had cycled early in that century. Note that various 'authorities' sometimes differ as to the etymology or 'first' use of a particular word or phrase. With the online availability of digitised newspapers, books and other materials, continuing research should enable clarification. However, in some instances it has only seemed to add confusion.

'Bicycle' was used in England at least as early as September 1868; some say it was derived from the French 'bicyclette' (1847) though some French sources suggest that 'bicyclette' was in fact adapted from the English word. The term 'cycle' was used by February 1870 and 'bike' as early as 1882, though it is not clear whether of American or English origin. 'Boneshaker' was quickly adopted to refer to the iron-rimmed, rough-riding velocipedes of the 1860s, and the term 'header' already in use by horsemen became popular as cyclists found themselves thrown forward off their high wheelers (sometimes fatally so). High wheelers were also referred to as 'ordinaries' and 'penny-farthings'. All of these words were in use not long afterward in Australia.

Some extremely popular expressions taken up by cyclists during the 1890s that have not survived in present day use, or are uncommon, include 'scorcher' and 'crack', referring to a top-class cycle racer, 'inflators' for tyre pumps, and 'rational dress' or 'rationals' for bloomers. 'Jigger', referring to mechanical gadgets having a jerky motion, was a synonym for bicycle in America, but was used here generally only in reference to American bicycles.

'Pushbike' or 'push bike' has long been an extremely popular word for a bicycle in Australia, possibly even more so than 'bicycle' itself in many circles. The earliest printed record of the word was long thought to be from an English newspaper of June 1905, but was found in print in Traralgon, Victoria in August 1904, thanks to recent online research by Denis Gojack. The *Australian Pocket Oxford Dictionary* referred to 'pushbike' as a slang word. However, in my view the term is so common in Australia—both today and in the past—that it could hardly be considered as 'peculiar to one class of people', or 'outside of standard English', the *Australian Pocket Oxford Dictionary*'s own definitions of slang. The word is used in England but is virtually unknown in the United States. One recent online bicycle forum, for example, had various Americans enquiring about the term pushbike and whether anyone had ever heard of it. An Australian eventually set them straight. Because of the increasing tendency to use the terms 'bike' and 'cycle' to refer to motor cycles, pushbike remains in wide use.

A number of words and phrases associated with the bicycle appear to be peculiarly Australian, such as 'getting off his bike', in the sense of losing one's temper, as used in Alan Seymour's *The One Day of the Year*: 'Awright, don't get orf yr bike!' Another is the reference to a sexually willing or promiscuous girl as a 'bike', the 'town bike' or 'office bike'. As David Williamson wrote in 1972 in *The Removalists*, 'Turned out the tart was the biggest bike in the district'.

The first adjustable handlebars seen on a bicycle by many Australians were those used by 'Major' Taylor, the legendary black American cycle

It is about 10 mm (nearly half an inch) between the points of a mature Emex australis

racer who toured Australia in 1903-04. For the next several decades the phrase 'Major Taylors' was commonly used in this country as a synonym for adjustable handlebars.

In his book *On the Wool Track* C.E.W. Bean referred to a man who 'nearly punctured getting up that bank' (wore himself out). However, the use of the word in that sense was not listed in Edward Morris's *Austral English* in 1898, English slang dictionaries of the era, nor later Australian language studies or dictionaries.

Sydney Baker, in his 1945 book *The Australian Language*, refers to the phrase 'bicycle bum' as an Australian adaptation of the American term 'bum', which refers to a tramp, hobo, or dissolute person; he did not indicate when the phrase came into use in this country.

'Grid' is also indicated as a slang word for 'bicycle' in English and Australian dictionaries, but the origin or evolution of the meaning to refer to bicycles is not at all clear. The term persisted as popular slang in many Australian schools until at least the late 1950s.

'Treadley' (spelled variously, e.g. treadly, tredly, treadlie, etc.) was and remains a colloquial term in Australia to refer to bicycles, and is noted as such in the Australian *Macquarie Online Dictionary*. However, it is not listed at all in the American *Merriam-Webster* or *Oxford* online dictionaries (for either 'British and World English' or 'US English' versions).

An especially interesting perspective upon colloquial Australian English is offered by cyclists' concerns with punctures from the numerous thorny plants found about the Australian countryside. The popular names of the plants were, and still are, confusing, misleading and inconsistently used both locally and nationally. For example, the most common plant that affected rural cyclists nationwide was *Emex australis*. It was apparently introduced from South Africa, first to Western Australia, where the Afrikaans word for it, *duweltjie* (devil's thorn) was corrupted to 'doublegee'. Other terms used to refer to it (both in WA and the eastern colonies) were 'prickly jack', 'three-cornered jack', 'Cape Spinach', 'Tanner's curse', 'giant bull head', and 'bendei' (spelled variously, e.g. 'bindy-eye', 'bindi-eye'). However, 'bendei' is routinely used to describe various species of both *Bassia* and *Emex*, which are not related to one another.

The widespread use of the bicycle on the Western Australian goldfields resulted in several words being adapted to the peculiar cycling circumstances found there, including 'pad' (which has a long history of referring to walking) for a bicycle path or camel track; 'special' 'special cyclist', or 'special rider' to refer to the cyclists who delivered messages about the goldfields; and 'lengthrunner' for the men who patrolled the Kalgoorlie water pipeline.

The Overlanders

Australia was the long-distance cycling centre of the world for many years. From late 1896 through mid-1900 some two dozen men undertook a series of widely publicised overland rides that convincingly demonstrated the cyclist's ability to traverse some of the harshest and most isolated parts of the continent. The motives varied. Some did it for the glory and others merely wanted to get from one place to another. The majority of the trips began in Western Australia and most of the riders had obtained cycling experience on the Western Australian goldfields.

Principal overland cycling routes

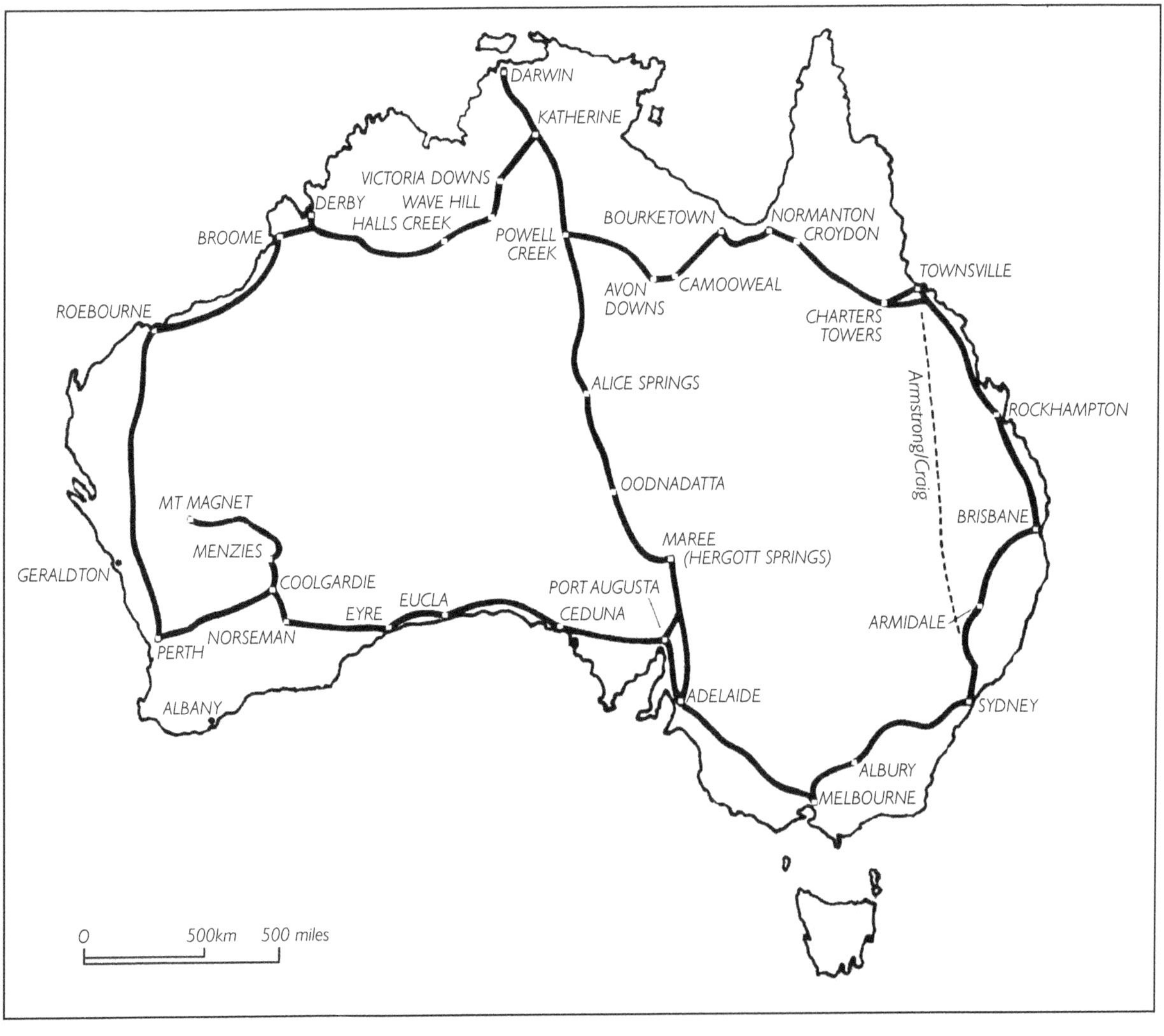

The Trans-Nullarbor

After Percy Armstrong completed his 1893 Croydon-to-Melbourne overland journey there was no other known transcontinental bicycle ride for three years. Then on 24 November 1896, at the start of the southern summer, Arthur Richardson pedalled out of Coolgardie, Western Australia toward Adelaide, intending to spend Christmas with his relatives. He was born in 1872 at Pernambuco, Brazil, one of ten children of a physician who soon afterward moved the family to Port Augusta, South Australia. Arthur attended Whinham College and Adelaide Collegiate School and served three years with the South Australian militia. By the mid-1890s his father was practising on the booming Western Australian goldfields and

Arthur Richardson, the first to cycle the Nullarbor (1896) and around Australia (1899-1900)

Arthur tried his hand at mining and station life. He was quiet, unassuming, highly independent and known for undertaking long walks on the goldfields simply to visit friends for an evening.

Carrying only a small kit and a waterbag, he followed the telegraph line much of the 2,100 kilometres (1,300 miles). He recalled much 'sweating and swearing' on sandy roads west of Eucla, suffered from hot winds and heat ('about 1000 in the shade') and judged the 24 miles (39 km) of sandhills west of Madura Station the 'worst in Australasia'. Nonetheless he arrived in Adelaide thirty-one days later, the first man to ride across the Nullarbor. The journey was widely reported in Australian newspapers and magazines and clearly demonstrated the value of the bicycle for long distance rural travel.

A few months later, in 1897, William Snell also undertook the ride. He was early on the scene in the Western Australian goldfields, a skilled bushman and camel handler, and according to one newspaper 'just what a long-distance rider should be: the impersonification of health and strength'. He completed the 3,000 kilometres (1,860 miles) from Menzies, north of Coolgardie, all the way to Melbourne in only 28 days, the second man to pedal across the Nullarbor. Originally from Hamilton, Victoria, Snell had pedalled east to get married and returned to the west soon afterwards (he did not require his bride to pedal back—they took the boat). He opened a shop in Menzies and was a pioneering figure in the Leonora district, serving six years as the municipality's first mayor. Billy Snell was highly popular and respected for his ability to raise money for various town projects. When he moved north in 1907 the *Leonora Miner* recognised his financial and cycling talents in a poem whose quality can be most graciously described as well-intentioned:

> Goodbye Billy I must leave you
> On your bike to sally forth,
> Something tells me I must grieve you
> When you travel to the North.
> Now if we write to the Departments
> They'll say we can go to 'ell,
> If you want any money Leonora
> Send down Billy Snell.

In 1942 he died in the bush northeast of Wiluna and his body was found some weeks later.

The Story of Australian Cycling

Billy Snell

Snell was soon followed by prospectors Fred and Bert James, who left Mount Magnet to return to their home in Geelong, Victoria, taking 48 days for the 3,500 kilometre (2,200 mile) ride.

In September William Virgin, a diminutive cycle express messenger rider at 5 feet 3½ inches (1.6 m) and 121 pounds (55 kg), left Perth for Brisbane. He arrived sixty days later to acclaim for the longest single ride yet undertaken in Australia (4,300 km, 2,700 miles). His time was considerably slowed because heavy rains on the Darling Downs left roads nearly impassable, and he had to spend two days in Goulburn, NSW recuperating from a severe dog bite.

William Virgin

Frank White (centre, in light clothes) was given a send off by a Perth crowd on 9 May 1898

In 1898 Scotchy Wright and Jack Denning began a race from Perth. A broken chain out of Norseman ended Denning's effort and Wright, suffering from equipment troubles and illness, required 44 days to reach Melbourne. However, he prepared a map and route notes for subsequent riders.

On 9 May 1898 Frank White left Perth for Brisbane in an attempt to break Virgin's record. The next day Jack Denning also left Perth and the two engaged in a race across the continent that received widespread publicity and was followed in many newspapers on a day-to-day basis. They were ahead of the record at virtually every stage of the way and passed one another at various points. While in the lead Denning's ride abruptly ended with a fall and hospitalisation in Armidale, NSW. Frank White continued to Brisbane to break Virgin's record by several days and then continued on to Rockhampton, requiring only 62 days for the nearly 3,350 mile (5,400 km) ride. After resting several days he turned around and pedalled back to Perth, completing the 6,700 mile (10,800 km) return trip in five months. For Americans, imagine a San Diego–Washington, D.C.–Boston return ride, all of it variously on rough dirt roads, through much sand, and along mere bush tracks. For Europeans, think of travelling north from Istanbul to Moscow, west to Paris and south nearly to Rome—then riding it in reverse.

Three months later Pat O'Dea headed back east with support from a Western Australian manufacturer, the B & B Tire Company. Born in Foster, Victoria, Pat had sailed to Western Australia in 1892 at the age of 16 and spent six years gaining extensive cycling experience on the Murchison goldfields. He rode from Perth to Adelaide in the blistering time of 18½

Pat O'Dea

days, averaging 103 miles (166 km) per day across the Nullarbor. He continued on to Melbourne, raising his daily average for the entire crossing to 110 miles (177 km). He married in 1903 and spent the remainder of his life principally in prospecting and mining activities in Tasmania, eventually managing the Renison Associated Tin Mine. He cycled into his seventies and spent his last winters in Cairns, where he died in 1965 at the age of 89.

Across The Centre

The 1,960 miles (3,150 km) between Adelaide and Darwin, across the heart of Australia, proved to be generally more difficult than the trans-Nullarbor route and was physically and mentally testing. It included extensive stretches of sand, including some dune fields which required riders to carry or drag their machines across them. Vegetation ranged from arid scrubland to thick timber in the tropical north, where were also found marshlands, intermittent streams and flowing rivers with crocodiles. The southerly portion included meandering dry river beds and salt pans.

On 10 March 1897 Jerome J. Murif left Adelaide to attempt the first bicycle crossing. He rode in a pair of comfortable pyjamas with a clean spare

Jerome J. Murif

pair which he changed into before arriving at the telegraph and pastoral stations en route. He wore high-topped boots rather than shoes, to prevent sand getting inside as he pushed the bicycle across the extensive sand dunes and plains. Murif walked much of the 300 miles (483 km) south of Alice Springs, tacking back and forth across dunes, and judged that 'only after a heavy rainfall could much riding be done in those sandy districts'. Murif found that some sandy soils had a thin crust, resulting from previous rainfalls, which could be ridden with deflated tyres. However, since passing animals and wagons destroyed the crust he often had to meander in search of rideable remnants.

Dry lake beds furnished the smoothest natural riding surfaces on the Australian continent. Murif rode a 'splendidly smooth' clay flat for some twenty miles (32 km) toward the MacDonnell Ranges but had one of his worst spells when he had to carry his machine on his shoulder mile after mile through a soft, marshy lake. With fixed wheel bicycles cyclists could not backpedal to lift pedals out of the way of obstacles and his pedals and cranks took an occasional blow. Near the start of his journey, sandhills at Strangways forced him to ride between the rails of a train line. Despite its 'destructively sharp cornered' stone ballast and rough sleepers it was the lesser of two evils.

Murif's journey was deliberately slow (he spent a week touring the Alice Springs district, for example) and he took 74 days to negotiate the route. Long before he reached Darwin he was the subject of many telegraph reports from stations along the way and after it was disclosed that he had ridden a German 'Electra' bicycle, the brand's reputation was immeasurably enhanced in Australia.

Although he was the first to cross central Australia by bicycle, very little is known about Murif. Upon the completion of his journey he was described as a 34 year old Irishman who had spent many years in the Antipodes, with 'a delightful brogue, all the energy and intrepidity of his race, an experienced bushman, a certificated engineer, and in the prime of his life'. However, the surname Murif does not appear in either Ireland's Eircom or Telstra Australia's national phone directories today, and of Facebook's billion or so users only a handful have that surname, and they are from Indonesia. Other than a brief correspondence in 1898 with Essington Lewis (who became General Manager of the Broken Hill Proprietary Company in 1921 and whom Murif met during his overland ride) nothing else is known of him.

He seems to have popped up, ridden across Australia, and disappeared. In discussing his book *From Ocean to Ocean*, Murif complained to Lewis that 'between editing and publishing, such an awful botch was made of the work that I have declined to have anything to do with the printed book'.

By the time Murif reached Darwin a team of racing cyclists sponsored

Tom Coleman

by Dunlop Tyres and the Austral Cycle Agency was put together to break the 'slow' record. The first party, Tom Coleman and Charles Greenwood, left Darwin but abandoned the ride shortly afterwards when Greenwood fell ill. A replacement rider, A.W.B. Mather, arrived in Darwin and on 12 August 1897 left with Tom Coleman on the record attempt. Strong southerly headwinds faced them continually. As well, Mather was plagued with a broken fork and they were frequently separated as Coleman (whose machine performed faultlessly) attempted to push on to break the record. It was a rough journey. He had to tack back and forth across the linear sand dunes, and suffered a bad fall after catching a pedal on a log. He found himself 'ploughing through the soft, flour-like' dry bed of the Hugh River seven times in fourteen miles, as a result of its meandering course across the countryside, with its 'fine impalpable dust which made the nostrils and throat feel as if on fire'. He eventually fell ill and had to cut the telegraph wires to get help. At Oodnadatta, SA, Mather telegraphed that 'In all my experience I have never yet met such terrible going'. They broke the record by only a few days and given their financial and administrative support the

Albert MacDonald, the fourth man to cross central Australia by bicycle, absolutely shattered the previous Darwin-Adelaide record

attempt was considered an outright failure. To make matters worse Coleman was served with writs for £150 worth of repairs to the telegraph line, more than a year's pay for an average worker.

In 1898 Albert MacDonald, a telegrapher with several years experience in the Northern Territory, left Darwin on 22 August. He knew the route intimately and was fortunate in benefitting from tailwinds during the ride. Also, recent rain allowed him to ride extensive sandy areas that previous cyclists had been forced to push through. He rode, pushed and carried his bicycle along the 1,960 mile (3,150 km) route in only 29 days, far faster than anyone thought possible. MacDonald capped it off with a one-day 187 mile (300 km) ride into Adelaide, his main concern being to keep his feet on the fixed wheel pedals during high speeds attained on downhill stretches. He then continued on to Melbourne, completing the entire 3,750 kilometre (2,325 mile) journey in 34 days.

Around the Continent

In mid-1899 the last great overland cycling challenge was tackled—the 13,100 kilometre (8,120 mile) ride around Australia. (For Americans it would equate to a trip from San Diego up to Seattle, over to Boston, down to Miami and across to San Diego. For Europeans, imagine riding a complete circuit from Istanbul northwest to Paris, east to Moscow, then south to Istanbul—twice.)

Arthur Richardson, the first trans-Nullarbor cyclist, left Perth on 15 June and headed north in an attempt to be the first to ride around the continent. He carried 25 pounds (11.4 kg) of luggage and a pistol. Heavy rain slowed his progress in Western Australia, with some black-soil plains unrideable for several days. He had to push and carry his bicycle through much sand. Patsy Durack, one of the Europeans who opened up the rugged Kimberly region of northwest Australia, met Richardson near Victoria Downs as he came through. Patsy made only a few notes in his diary about the meeting, but the fact that the cyclist had covered 2,587 miles (4,165 km) since leaving Perth (Richardson had a cyclometer) was one of them. He was especially impressed by Richardson's ride from Wave Hill to Victoria Downs in two days, a 'worthy performance, knowing as I do the state of the road'.

Eight months later, on 4 February 1900, Arthur rode into Perth after

Soon after its completion, the story of Richardson's ride around Australia was recounted in a small book published by the Dunlop Pneumatic Tyre company. It included his reference to encountering 'hostile blacks' across the north of the continent

crossing southern Australia and the Nullarbor in the heat of summer. In doing so he completed the longest continuous cycle journey in the world to date. It was little heralded outside Australia and few who heard of it abroad would have appreciated the remote and harsh conditions under which much of the trip was made. In Australia, however, Richardson received considerable publicity and achieved a brief fame.

Just five weeks after completing his around-Australia ride he joined the Third (Bushmen's) Contingent from Western Australia and shipped out to the Boer War from Fremantle on 13 March 1900. A local cycle agent donated a bicycle for him to use as a scout or dispatch rider. The contingent disembarked at Beira, Mozambique on 18 April but Richardson broke his arm and left the service two months later near Salisbury, Rhodesia. Acording to a friend he worked on the West African coast for two years and then in various mining activities in South America before serving in the First World War. Arthur was badly wounded and spent two years in hospital at Rouen, France. He subsequently worked as an engineer in England, but his war injuries had left him seriously disturbed and in 1939 he shot and killed first his wife and then himself.

The more flamboyant Frank White admitted that he rode for the fame and deeply regretted that after riding from Perth to Rockhampton in 1898 he had turned around and reversed his route to Perth rather than continuing on around the continent. With the possibility that Richardson might not complete his circum-Australian effort, Frank left from Melbourne with his brother Alec in a counter-clockwise direction. In Brisbane Donald Mackay joined them. Frank White had to abandon his around-Australia effort when he suffered irreparable damage to his crank at Pine Creek, in the Northern Territory. The other two continued on without him while he made his way to Darwin to wait for a replacement. After repairs Frank had to console himself with a solo ride south to Port Augusta and across the Nullarbor to Perth. This, an extraordinary ride in itself, received little attention because it was a mere sidelight in the context of the circum-Australian efforts.

Alec White and Mackay eventually arrived in Perth just after Richardson had successfully completed his continental circuit. Donald Mackay determined to at least try and best Richardson's time of 243 days, which meant pedalling from Perth on to Brisbane in fifty days. He had hoped Frank White (who was waiting for Donald and Alec when they arrived in Perth) would go with him, as he had experience with the route.

This group of pioneer Australian cycling overlanders was photographed in Perth in mid-1899. It includes (l. to r.) Arthur Richardson; Percy Armstrong, by then Western Australia's leading cycle dealer; A.W.B. Mather, the Dunlop Tyre representative in Perth; and Frank White. Richardson and White would soon set off on separate attempts to become the first to ride around the continent

Frank went with him to Adelaide but stopped there, too weary to continue. Alec pedalled to the Victorian border with Donald before dysentery left him too weak to continue. Mackay travelled the rest of the way himself to set the round-Australia record of 240 days 7 hours. In fact Mackay had ridden further than Richardson as he had done a round trip from Katherine to Darwin (750 kilometres in all) to get some bicycle parts. However, Richardson received the greatest recognition by virtue of having been the first to complete the ride and having done so alone.

The overland journeys quickly sated the press and public and it took ever greater feats to sustain interest. By 1899 the Nullarbor crossing was considered to have lost its novelty and had become insignificant in comparison with the around Australia rides. After only five men had pedalled the Nullarbor, a journal opined that 'We appear to be having quite a procession of cyclists from Western Australia to Melbourne, and it looks as if the journey will ere long become quite popular amongst athletic cyclists

... a speed of 10 miles per hour can be fairly kept up, so that the road to the Golden West is not so terrible as it is generally thought'. Notwithstanding such views, the overland rides were not easy. The members of at least two parties who tried the journey nearly died of thirst and some riders refused to undertake subsequent rides on which they were invited. One stated flatly that he had 'had enough'.

Some were dubious about a few of the riders' motives, claiming their rides were undertaken merely to increase the sales of tyres and machines and benefited only the manufacturers and agents. Certainly there were grounds for this view. For example, after Murif, Coleman and Mather had required over two months to cross Australia via Alice Springs, MacDonald was rebuffed in his first efforts to have a bicycle donated for his attempt. The manager of the Austral Cycle Agency argued that if it required sixty days to do 2,000 miles (3,200 km), it could hardly be regarded as a test of the quality of the machine. What he really meant was that from a commercial perspective quality was synonymous with speed. With trans-Nullarbor cyclists covering nearly 1,800 miles (2,900 km) in three weeks, a trip of 2,000 miles (3,200 km) in over eight weeks was not a good advertisement. It was only when MacDonald promised to ride all the way to Melbourne from Darwin within 35 days that the Austral Cycle Agency agreed to help—but they acknowledged the arrangement and paid up only after successful completion. The commercialism surrounding some overlanders' rides led one writer to comment upon a non-sponsored effort: 'wonderful to relate, we do not know what tyres he uses, or what machine he rides, which is rather a relief'.

The early overland cyclists were not explorers of new country. All of the journeys were along routes previously traversed by migrants, prospectors, teamsters or bush workers. The manager of the Alice Springs telegraph station reported that during the months before Jerome Murif's maiden cycle journey through the centre, the route had been walked by several men looking for work, and another cyclist had ridden from Oodnadatta to Alice Springs nearly a year earlier. Arthur Richardson, on his round-Australia ride, received information about Western Australian and Northern Territory cycling conditions from J. Philips, who had just come across by bicycle from Croydon to Derby, the first man known to cross the 'top end' by bicycle. Like most rural travellers in remote areas they depended to some extent upon established properties, telegraph stations and teamsters for food and other assistance along the way. In some instances the aid was crucial to their survival. If the riders were courageous, considerable courage was unquestionably drawn from the fact that a place to rest and restock was rarely more than 100 miles (160 km) away, and they had the benefit of others' knowledge of the route. For example, while crossing the Nullarbor in 1894 a traveller had mapped ten rock holes, two tanks, two homesteads and a well along the 164-mile (264 km) route between the Eucla telegraph station and the Eyre homestead. As Jerome Murif emphasised, 'The cyclist who is sure of his road can never imagine the weakening effect which uncertainties on that most vital point can produce. Such doubts evolve sickening, depressing, unhappy sensations which make themselves felt more acutely than do the mere bodily disablements associated with hunger and thirst.'

In the 20th century overland rides continued but with much less publicity than previously. The line between an overland ride and merely a long trip became less distinguishable or relevant as innumerable riders covered thousands of miles annually in their wanderings. John Miles, who eventually discovered the mineral potential of Mount Isa, pedalled an unheralded 1,500 miles (2,400 km) from Broken Hill to North Queensland in six weeks in 1908, the same year that Fred Blakeley and the O'Neill brothers rode to Darwin from White Cliffs, NSW. The Cape York Peninsula was cycled by 1910 and after the Canning Stock Route was marked in 1907 it too was cycled. Newspaper files indicate that through the 1930s the Nullarbor was being crossed annually by scores of known riders, and personal diaries suggest that many more unreported travellers bicycled across.

Long distance rides by rural cyclists were no longer newsworthy, but they were not any easier than for those who had gone before. In 1902 the Reverend A. Sussex accompanied a cyclist from Lawlers to Mount Magnet,

Donald and Porteous, being sponsored by Western Australian manufacturers, and not out to break any records, received little national publicity

WA, because 'for one thing, he could not tolerate the loneliness of the road'. Fred and Bert James, speaking of their Nullarbor crossing in 1897, summed it up well: 'At times the vast solitude of the desert had a depressing effect on us, the whirring of the bikes and an occasional glimpse of the telegraph line alone reminding us we were still on the face of the earth'.

Some occasional overland rides were still of interest to the general newspaper readers. One was in 1914 when Eddie Reichenbach managed to break the Darwin-Adelaide record, set by Albert MacDonald sixteen years before, by some fifteen hours. Hubert Opperman's 13-day sprint from Fremantle to Sydney via Melbourne in 1937 was widely followed but was not in the realm and spirit of the early overlanders. Opperman had accompanying motor vehicle support from Bruce Small and his Malvern Star bicycle company, with its intense publicity machine. In a conversation with him in the late 1970s Oppy told me that Bruce would have him take a break ostensibly to sleep for four or five hours only to wake him up in a couple of hours. He said he fell asleep and off his bike several times. Though he held virtually all Australian inter-city records in his day, he laughed when I informed him that he had not broken Frank White's Perth–Rockhampton record: 'I didn't know there was one or I would have!'

The early overlanders' travels, widely reported throughout Australia, were important in publicising the speed and feasibility of bicycle use in the outback. When Frank White returned to Perth from Rockhampton he was escorted into Perth and the police had to clear the streets to allow him to reach the G.P.O. He received a medal and newspapers carried a several-column feature article on the trip. 'Journeys such as this, although somewhat dangerous, are far more useful than races as demonstrations of what a truly wonderful machine the modern bicycle is, and what long and rough journeys it enables men to accomplish'.

However, the overlanders' fame was relatively short-lived. For one thing the nature of the rides left them outside the commonly conceived realm of bicycle sports or racing. And the fact that they were never really the first to go anywhere meant that they earned no place in the tableau of Australian exploration history either. That's unfortunate, for they comprise a truly remarkable episode in the history of Australians adopting technology to overcome transport difficulties. If one function of an explorer is to demonstrate possibilities to those that follow, then certainly the overland cyclists were explorers in Australia's transport history.

Francis Birtles

No story of Australian outback travel and exploration is complete without mentioning Francis Birtles and his three-decade career as a one-of-a-kind overland cyclist, photographer, filmmaker, writer and motorist extraordinaire. Birtles was the product of an era when adventure and fame

Francis Birtles, 1912

could be found in accomplishing ever quicker and more daring journeys by bicycle and motor car. He cycled across the continent several times and pedalled around it completely. He pioneered the outback travel-adventure film—by bicycle—and was the first to drive a car from London to Melbourne, as well as making numerous other motor crossings of the continent.

Born in 1881, Birtles joined the merchant navy when fifteen. In 1899, during the Boer War, he jumped ship in Cape Town and served two and a half years in a troop of irregular mounted infantry. After the war he spent a further two years as a mounted police officer in the Transvaal. His brief war writings demonstrate his early flair for describing events and places: '... vultures, gorged to capacity, flop-flopped and rose heavily on lazily beating wings against the yellow dawn. The air that we breathed as we rode on, mile after mile, was polluted with the odour of week-old, jackal-torn carcasses of horses which had met with cruel lingering deaths in a disastrous running skirmish of several days before. Some of the former veldt riders were now sleeping peacefully beneath scattered earth mounds'.

In South Africa he acquired extensive bush survival skills, undertook cycling excursions in harsh, arid environments, and developed expertise with photography. By 1905 it 'occurred to me that my own country offered opportunities for hard living and adventurous exploits'. He returned to Australia to undertake a series of outback travels that occupied him for the next thirty years.

It was Boxing Day of 1905 when Birtles disembarked at Fremantle. He pedalled out of Perth to Kalgoorlie, then headed northeast from the goldfields towards Alice Springs, but the intense summer heat of the desert and scarcity of water turned him back. Turning south and then east, he crossed the Nullarbor. Over the next six years he became the most peripatetic cycling overlander in Australian history. As Birtles rode his bicycle about the continent he photographed its wonders, himself among them, and wrote about his adventures.

His first book, *Lonely Lands*, was published in 1909 with 224 pages and 85 photographs, and set the pattern for his later writings—a wealth of pictures of strange things in isolated places, together with tales of the difficulties he met on the journey. His early photographs show him wearing shorts, a South African style of dress not to be common in Australia for many years. He financed his passion by writing several magazine articles and books between 1910 and 1912, and the major retailer Anthony Horden

Wheeling Matilda

Francis Birtles with his camera in camp

and Sons provided him with a 'Universal' bicycle in exchange for his endorsement.

Birtles' travels are remarkable for the sheer physical effort and mental determination involved in pedalling tens of thousands of miles in the bush with massive loads on the machine. In 1911, with a French Gaumont Film Company cinematographer, Richard Primmer, he rode 4,000 kilometres (6,500 m) from Sydney to Darwin. It was an epic trip in terms of logistics. They carried still cameras, a stereoscopic camera, cinematographic camera, photographic plates, film, and developing tanks and fluids. A contemporary observer estimated they carted about 250 pounds of professional equipment, split between them, plus food, water and personal camping gear.

The film, *Across Australia,* was released in Sydney in May 1912. It was some 3,000 feet long and included scenes of emus, crocodile hunting, sugar cane growing, pearling on Thursday Island, and shark fishing. Contemporary accounts lauded the film, 'showing places never before seen by a Sydney audience', and it played to a crowd which 'thronged the Lyceum'. In July that same year it ran in Melbourne and Adelaide. Birtles' personal film debut had in fact occurred three months before, in a Gaumont gazette film: He was photographed arriving in Sydney on 1 February 1912, at the end of his last overland cycle ride.

He took up motoring about the bush with the same enthusiasm he had for bicycles and immediately made the first west-east motor crossing of Australia. He always carried a bicycle as 'a lifeboat'. In late September 1927, with support from Shell and Dunlop, he left London in a Bean car, the *Sundowner*, bound for Australia. Farewelled from Australia House in London, he faced poor roads, scarce supplies and daunting terrain. Birtles reached Melbourne in mid-1928, the first ever to motor the route. The feat was so challenging that it was not repeated until 1955. The journey was widely reported, very difficult (he was hospitalized in India), and his observation of Baghdad crowds is pure Birtles: 'A swarm of guides and mendicants surrounded the car. I recognised them as the descendants of the Forty Thieves, but they had multiplied exceedingly!'

In 1935 Birtles published his second and final book, *Battle Fronts of Outback*, and effectively retired. He died of heart disease in New South Wales in July 1941, proud that his 'expeditions with pen and camera had

Birtles' last overland cycle journey ends in Sydney, 1912

Francis Birtles, 1923

helped to make the interior a reality to the general consciousness' of the nation. By then the outback was a different place from when Birtles had first explored it, with the pedal wireless radio and airplanes making Schools of the Air and the Royal Flying Doctor Service possible, and motor vehicles enabling widespread travel and easier and cheaper provision of goods and services. Through his forays he had introduced such exotic Australian places as Darwin, Broome, Derby, and Wyndham to a generation of readers and theatre-goers. Within seven months they would become household words, along with Pearl Harbor, Bataan and Singapore. His passing truly marked the end of an outback era.

Donald Mackay

Donald Mackay, powerfully built and physically fit, was the rich man's Francis Birtles. Born of Scottish parents at Yass, New South Wales in 1870, he grew up on the family property and received a very large inheritance after his father died in 1890. A self-described 'descendant of the wandering Jew', Mackay travelled to a number of countries, bicycled around the Australian continent, and privately funded an exploratory expedition to New Guinea and a series of land explorations and aerial surveys of central and northern Australia. In 1942 Frank Clune published a book on Mackay's life, including a detailed account of his around-Australia ride.

Mackay took trips abroad to New Zealand in 1890 and China and Japan in 1892. Upon his return from a short trip to Europe in 1897 he realised 'more than ever what a jolly fine place Australia is'. Aside from his travels, much of the 1890s was spent working and travelling in western New South Wales seeking opals and gold. In the process he cycled some 2,000 miles (3,200 km).

When Arthur Richardson began his highly publicised bicycle ride around Australia Mackay considered the possibility of doing a similar ride himself. When he heard about Frank White's proposed effort Mackay made contact with him. Frank agreed to have Donald join him and his brother Alec on the journey. Mackay linked up with the pair in Brisbane. After a day's rest the three of them set out on Monday, 30 July 1899. Among Mackay's gear were two water cans, a set of tools and bicycle parts, waterproof rain cloak, diary, food bag, revolver and a camera. Clune's book contains fifty photographs taken by Mackay during a lifetime of exploits, however there were none from this ride.

Mackay had done no bicycle riding for the previous month while arranging his affairs, and was, at 196 pounds (89 kg), a good fourteen pounds (6 kg) overweight. The White brothers, in superb condition, helped Donald the first few days by massaging his legs until the trip ceased to be a 'purgatorial ordeal'. Because of extremely heavy rains it took seven days to cover the first 350 miles to Rockhampton, and they had to alternately ride and push the bicycles alongside or on the railway line much of the way.

The rides of Richardson and the White brothers/Mackay trio were highly publicised nationally with their progress being monitored by telegraphic and newspaper reports. As a result they were welcomed by both cyclists and

Donald Mackay

non-cyclists in the towns, small communities, and properties they passed through. They would often be escorted into and out of towns by local cycle club members and the general public, sometimes numbering in the dozens.

In one community a cricket match was stopped so that the players and the crowd could greet and cheer them. Festivities were held for them when they stayed overnight or stopped for lunch, whether in large towns or small bush pubs. While gratifying, the insistence upon celebrating with dances and musical gatherings for the visitors late into the night posed occasional problems as they simply wished to have a quiet rest and sleep. In Charleston, the entire population of thirty 'rough and bearded males' gathered and took turns playing an accordion until midnight, 'some excellent in melody and rhythm, some just wheezy'. In one case they were taken to a cockfight, which Mackay found 'a sickening exhibition'. But as the three depended upon local people for support, particularly in the more remote areas, it was one of the dues to be paid for cycling celebrity.

During the ride they slept in abandoned stockmen's huts, teamsters' shanties 'of the roughest sort', on verandas, in hotels of less than sterling quality, at teamsters' and railway navvies' camps, and on the ground, scraping a hiphole if the ground was soft or sandy enough. They looked forward to and appreciated the occasional hot bath, shave, dinner and good bed. To save weight they carried few provisions in the more settled areas, buying food and meals each day. On long runs they survived on dried meat, flour and tea. A police officer west of Camooweal killed and baked a goat to provide them with adequate food for a long stretch ahead in which no supplies would be available. However they occasionally arrived at a police outpost or other remote spot in which there was not sufficient food for them.

Along the Queensland coast and in the Northern Territory they had to strip and wade across numerous streams and rivers and carry their machines through muddy or swampy conditions 'for many weary miles'. It must be remembered that carrying the bike meant carrying everything on it as well, a total of about 75 pounds (35 kg) to be shouldered. A writer for *The Northern Territory Times* commented that the ability of the bicycle to manage such a heavy load plus rider was commendable, but it 'would take a lot of the gilt off the gingerbread when it came to reversing the order of things—the man carrying the bike'. A few miles out of Charters Towers, after a heavy rain, the black soil plains were so cloying that the bikes had to be carried for several hours with the walkers stopping frequently to cut the heavy mud off their boots with knives. They had to push their machines over a rough track across the Stockman's Range, with its basalt boulders and steep descents and across the 'top end' of Australia much of the travel between cattle stations was not on formed roads at all but along rough wagon or cattle tracks. They suffered occasional punctures, broken spokes and bent or buckled wheels, which had to be repaired and re-aligned.

The three typically covered about fifty miles per day through northern and western Queensland. They were fortunate to be riding not only in the dry season, but during a drought in which most streams around the Gulf of Carpentaria had little or no water to be crossed. However, the drought also meant there was no water in places it would normally be found. West of Camooweal they ran out of water and nearly died of thirst after being severely slowed by rough roads, getting lost at one stage, and having to stop for Alec, who had severe dysentery, to rest. Frank pushed on to the overland telegraph station at Powell's Creek and sent back two stockmen to rescue his companions. The three averaged only 27 miles per day over that section.

At Powell's Creek they met Arthur Richardson, their round-Australia rival. All four cyclists rested there for three days until Alec had recovered from the dysentery and was fit to continue. During that time they exchanged detailed information about the routes each had ridden. Richardson then headed east and the trio north to Darwin, suffering particularly badly from mosquitoes at the various water holes along the way. They had arranged for tyres and other sundries to be shipped to Darwin but nothing had arrived. They managed to get two new inner tubes each and some rubber solution from a local business but no new tyres. After overhauling the machines they headed back south to Katherine whence they would pedal west into the most difficult, isolated portion of the journey. However, on the way south Frank's crank broke at Pine Creek, could not be repaired, and he had to abandon the ride. He would have to wait for a replacement to be shipped up to Darwin.

Alec and Donald set out on the 900-mile ride to Derby, among the most sparsely settled areas of the continent. The isolation of the route is difficult to appreciate today. Halls Creek, the only 'settlement' between Katherine and Derby, had only a handful of permanent residents. Otherwise there were only scattered cattle stations, the first having been opened up less than two decades before. As Frank Clune wrote, the cattlemen were 'encroaching on the territory of the wild black tribes, who are still resisting this invasion of their ancestral demesnes. War between pioneers and blacks—a war of rifle and revolver versus spear and waddy—was still raging. When the blacks

The Story of Australian Cycling

Alec and Frank White, circa 1900. Alec White was the second man to pedal around Australia. His brother Frank, who organised the ride, failed to complete it because of mechanical troubles

speared a white man it was murder; and when the whites shot the blacks in scores it was revenge... On principle, white men shot at blacks on sight, to teach them a lesson and to keep them at a distance'. At Newcastle Waters Station in the Northern Territory Donald noted that a dozen rifles were kept on racks and a pack of dogs to give warning of any hostile approach. The pair of cyclists kept their pistols handy and used them on a couple of occasions to scare away blacks who threw spears at them. When they reached Derby, the small port on the west coast which provided supplies and communication with the outside world, the cyclists found only a dozen houses and two pubs. The case was similar for most of the 'towns' down the Western Australian coast.

The cyclists were welcome visitors at the cattle stations and provided with food and rest. At Flora Valley Station near the Western Australian border they had to stop and wrap their deteriorating tyres with green hide— untanned calf skin—which they soaked in water, then stretched and lashed around the tyres. After a few hours in the sun it dried and shrank, making a strong cover. The pair averaged only 27 miles per day for the 900 miles to Derby as much of the route had at best only cart or animal tracks. One of Alec's tubes had a slow leak and since the green hide could not be removed for repair they had to stop frequently and pump it up. At Halls Creek they managed to get some spare canvas to re-wrap the tyre, and in Derby were able to pick up new tyres they had arranged to have waiting there.

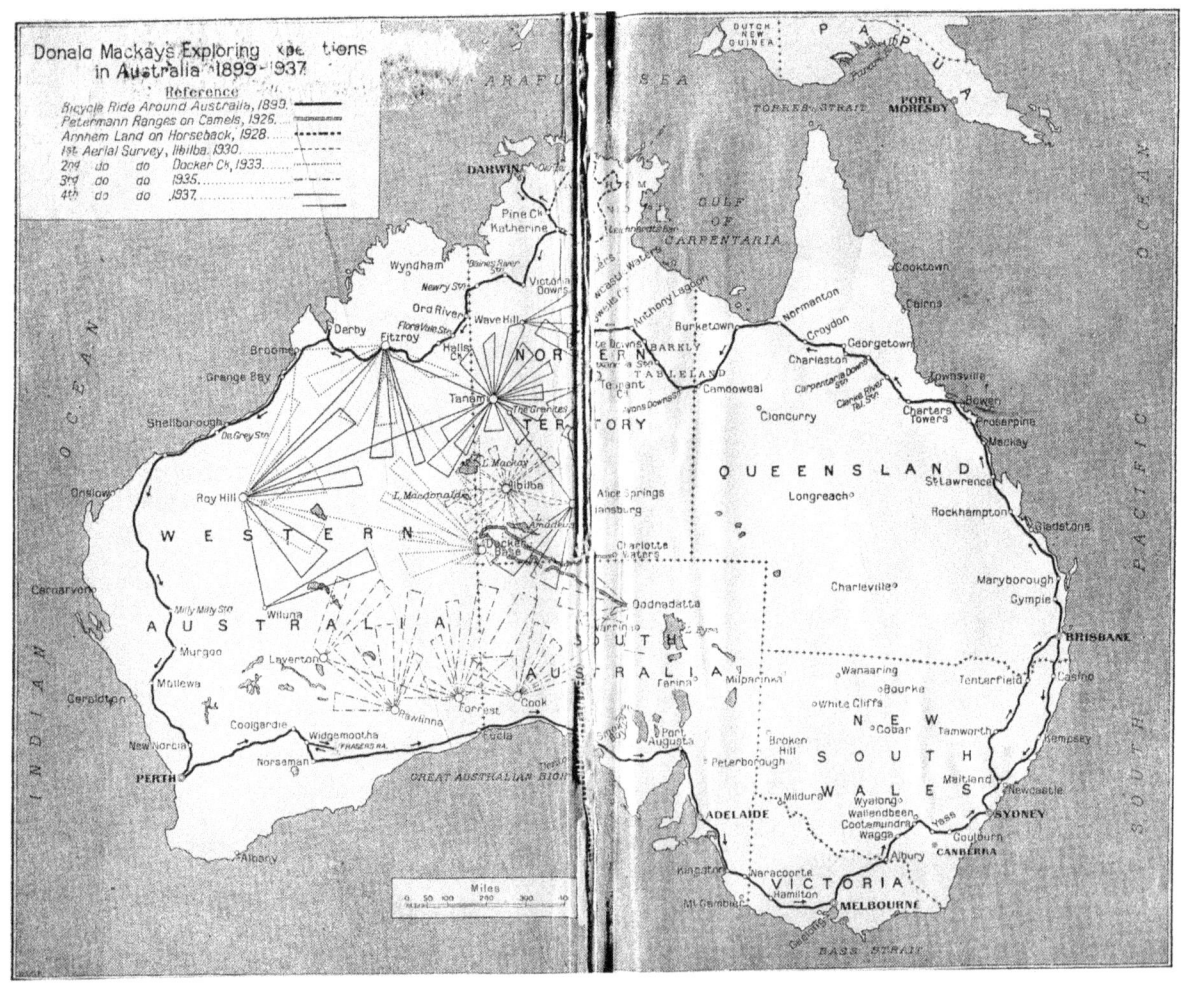

Map reproduced from the front endpaper of Last of the Explorers, Frank Clune's 1942 biography of Donald Mackay, showing his bicycle route, anthropological expeditions, and aerial surveys

Marble Bar, Western Australia, date unknown

The run south from Derby involved tremendous distances on sandy roads. They were able to pedal on firm sand along 80 Mile Beach but eventually had to turn inland and faced extremely difficult going. The nearly completed telegraph line, cattle stations, and small mining communities meant little further worry about food and supplies. However, they were heading into the peak of the summer and the hottest part of the continent. They passed within 100 km (62 miles) of the mining community of Marble Bar, which holds the world record of 160 consecutive days of 100 °F (40 °C) or above. During December and January temperatures in excess of 45 °C (113 °F) are common, and for half the year the average maximum temperature exceeds normal human body temperature. Understandably, the 1,500 mile (2,400 km) route from Derby to Perth was 'six weeks of sweat, sand and sorrow'.

At New Norcia, 130 kilometres (80 miles) north of Perth, the pair were surprised to find Frank White waiting for them. He had ridden from Darwin south to Adelaide and across the Nullarbor to Perth. They were met with the news that Arthur Richardson arrived in Perth two days before, having completed the first cycling circumnavigation of the continent. As indicated previously, Donald went on to actually break Richardson's round-Australia record and was given a silver trophy by the Dunlop Tyre Company 'in recognition of his meritorious cycle ride around Australia'.

While Mackay was fortunate to experience not a single day's illness nor serious injury at any time during the ride—unlike Alec who occasionally suffered severe dysentery for days, and mild dysentery for weeks—the hardships were considerable and he had come within hours of dying of thirst in the Northern Territory. But in the end, 'Yes, it had been worth while'.

Culturally they met an array of people on the journey. In Queensland they watched indentured South Sea Islanders labouring in the sugarcane fields. Near the Queensland-Northern Territory border they met Chinese who were trying to sneak across into Queensland without paying the poll tax the colony had instituted to try and keep the 'celestials' out. Blacks ranged from the two who rescued them in the Northern Territory to those throwing spears at them in the Northern Territory-Western Australia border region. At one wayside shanty in Queensland they walked in to find three uniformed Salvation Army men, who had just pedalled some 60 miles, slaking their thirst with beer, temperance principles notwithstanding. That was not surprising for alcohol and alcoholism were common elements in the isolated communities and properties through which they passed.

During the course of his 1899-1900 cycle ride Donald Mackay gained invaluable experience about travelling and living in the harsh, remote outback, and began to envision an expedition to explore Central Australia, much of which was still unknown to Europeans. In 1908-09 he managed and financed a large expedition to explore the Purari River region northwest of Port Moresby, New Guinea (during which he suffered malaria and serious infections).

In 1925 he initiated and funded a plan to explore the Petermann Ranges southwest of Lake Amadeus. Only a handful of Europeans had ever seen this region and the member of one exploration party had been speared to death by hostile aborigines. Mackay invited Herbert Basedow, one of Australia's great anthropologists, to join him. Basedow had extensive experience in working in Central Australia since 1905 and knowledge of at least two aboriginal languages. With two experienced bushmen to handle camels and general chores they set off from Oodnadatta, South Australia in May 1926 with wireless equipment and photographic and sound recording gear. Over a three-month period they recorded various indigenous songs, took many photographs, and explored the Petermann Ranges and previously unexplored country to the north. They walked much of the journey as they mapped, climbed and measured peaks. The expedition contributed important ethnographic information, pictures and audio recordings.

Purari River village, New Guinea

In 1928 Basedow and Mackay explored Arnhem Land, the hot tropical region east of Darwin (from which they took the train south to Katherine, 29 years after Mackay had bicycled the route). Mackay's notes on the Railway Hotel in Katherine were 'many drunks–bedroom has stale sheets—no water or candle—bed stinks—lie on top—red hot—few mosquitoes—drunks singing and are sick'. Over a two-month period their small party and pack team of horses covered some 700 miles (1,100 km). A chapter title from Clune's book sums it up: 'Mosquitoes, Mud and Misery'. Mackay suffered a septic hand, his entire arm being inflamed and the harsh conditions triggered tension between Donald and Basedow. Nonetheless, for Basedow it was 'his most important piece of zoological and anthropological research', made possible by Mackay.

In 1930 Mackay personally financed and supervised a series of four aerial surveys over the next seven years that would revolutionise knowledge

Wheeling Matilda

Airplane and camels at Ilbilba, 1930

about the interior of the country. About one-third of the continent, in central and western Australia, was unoccupied by Europeans and only a few explorers had even crossed it. Mackay's first survey, in 1930, was based at Ilbilba, in the southwest of the Northern Territory. There was no aerodrome so pack camels carried twelve tons of equipment and supplies from 250 miles (400 km) away and an advance team cleared a 700-yard (640 m) square landing area and kept a smoke fire burning so the planes could find the airstrip when they arrived.

Fifteen flights were carried out in 24 days, photographing and mapping the country. Just how unexplored Australia still was at the time is no better emphasised than by noting that Lake Mackay (named in Donald's honour) was discovered during the initial survey. Unknown to Europeans, it was found to be Australia's second largest lake. In America it would rank only behind the five Great Lakes and the Great Salt Lake in size. Far more extensive aerial surveys were undertaken in 1933, 1935 and 1937.

Donald Mackay was awarded an O.B.E. in 1934 and C.B.E. in 1937, and acknowledged as 'the last Australian explorer'. He died in September 1958, a widower with no children.

Ted Ryko/Eddie Reichenbach

Edward Reichenbach, later to be known as Ted Ryko, first came to public attention in 1914 when he broke Albert MacDonald's sixteen year old Darwin to Adelaide cycling record. He was born of German immigrants in 1892 near Nhill in Victoria. An avid photographer, he left a legacy in his photographic record of people and life in central and northern Australia. He was also an amateur botanist and naturalist, contributing to notable collections of plant specimens.

When a young man he travelled widely, using a bicycle while servicing equipment for his uncle's engineering firm. He met John Flynn (who would later found the Royal Flying Doctor Service) in Wagga Wagga in about 1913

and had the opportunity to read some of the diaries which described Flynn's experiences in central Australia where he headed the Australian Inland Mission and ministered to a huge area. Eddie was inspired and encouraged by Flynn and developed an interest in the region.

He was also motivated by Francis Birtles' rides and in 1914 set out to best the Darwin-Adelaide overland record. In reverse direction to MacDonald's 1898 solo ride south from Darwin, Reichenbach headed north from Adelaide with a friend, Jack Fahey. Eddie's bicycle had reinforced front forks, wheels with especially strong spokes, Dunlop Thorn Proof tyres and a three-speed freewheel hub with rim brakes. MacDonald had used a standard fixed wheel machine—freewheels weren't yet available—with no brakes. Eddie also mounted a small acetylene lamp with a gas generating plant attached to the frame of the bicycle and sent supplies of carbide ahead to the telegraph stations along the route.

Eddie and Fahey set out in May 1914. Not far into the ride Jack injured a leg or ankle and had to slowly make his way north, leaving Reichenbach on his own. On most days Eddie continued into the night since the winter days were short and the track heavy going. Nights were cold and Eddie would assemble a wind break and build a small fire, both to protect himself from the cold and to minimise body moisture condensation inside his rubberised sleeping bag. Along the route he made mail deliveries to isolated homesteads in return for a 'good feed' and a few hours lodging.

Reichenbach's camera was an essential part of his equipment and he took some 200 photographs in all during the journey—of his bicycle, riding surfaces, people, and natural features along the way. Once while he was setting up his machine for a photograph on the Finke River his bicycle was swept downstream, the tyres and his luggage providing enough buoyancy to keep it floating. He had to strip off and dive in to rescue it. With all his gear wet and night descending he sprinkled carbide on some dry leaves and lit a fire by discharging his revolver. He was thus able to dry out his equipment and keep warm.

Eddie Reichenbach broke MacDonald's record by fifteen hours, completing the 1,969-mile (3,169 km) journey in 28 days and 7 minutes. He received £50 from Dunlop, a substantial portion of a worker's annual income at the time. In addition Dunlop advertised the ride widely, among other things placing a full-page advertisement in *The Bulletin* that included eighteen of Reichenbach's photographs.

The Story of Australian Cycling

The camera did much to promote cycle touring in the 1890s and early 20th century. The photographic album, Glimpses of Australia, *was advertised in the New South Wales Cycling Gazette in 1896. The man pictured above was photographed in the Northern Territory in 1897 by A. W. B. Mather, during his Darwin to Adelaide ride*

After arriving in Darwin Reichenbach eventually set up a photography business in a shop on Cavanagh Street. A contemporary who first met him at Pine Creek during his overland ride said he was 'one of the most energetic and capable men I know. He made frequent trips ... cycling hundreds of miles across country carrying his camera and necessaries with him. He thought nothing of taking trips of 600 or 700 miles'. His travels provided material for a regular column called 'Territory Jottings', for *The Northern Territory Times and Gazette* (commonly referred to as *The Northern Territory Times*). He produced postcards from his photographs—of buffalo hunting, cattle droving, aboriginal people and their traditional hunting and ceremonies, missionaries, buildings and natural features—with his bicycle often appearing in the photograph. He seems to have spent time around Coburg Peninsula and Goulburn and Melville Islands, as well as Borroloola. There is evidence of close contact with the Tiwi people and he was also known to the Warrawi (Goulburn Island) community. An aboriginal rock painting in the Wellington Ranges of Arnhem Land records an encounter with the young photographer and his bicycle.

Unfortunately both Eddie and his surname were victims of First World War prejudice. With patriotism running high, many people, towns and streets had their Germanic names changed. In NSW for example, Germanton was considered unpatriotic and the town was renamed Holbrook. Amidst this nationalistic fervour Eddie changed his surname to Ryko, but still suffered. Although born in Australia, intelligence officials were suspicious of his photographic excursions. Possibly a contributing factor was the recent death of German-born Paul Foelsche, a long-time Darwin resident who had travelled widely about the Territory taking hundreds of photographs of the land and its aborigines. Foelsche died on January 31 1914, just five months before Reichenbach pedalled into town with his camera. Two months later war broke out. With spy fever rampant in Australia that was perhaps a bit too much of a coincidence for suspicious minds, given that

the northeastern portion of New Guinea, across the Arafura Sea, was in the hands of Germany at the outbreak of the war. Ryko's premises were raided and he was constantly harassed to the point where he left Darwin in 1917.

Ryko went to Sydney, then Melbourne to tour rural Victoria with a "Win the War" candidate, addressing gatherings on life and conditions in the Northern Territory. He married in 1920 and had a son two years later. His movements over the next two decades are uncertain, though he appears to have spent time in Queensland and reportedly worked on construction of the Sydney Harbour Bridge. Around 1940 he began working with the Commonwealth Railways at Katherine River and was in charge of the water pumping station at Bundooma by the time he retired in 1957. During those years he became a well-respected naturalist and amateur botanist. After retiring from the Railways in 1957 he was diagnosed with Parkinson's disease and returned to live at his immigrant parents' home, Glenlee, in Victoria. He died in September 1968, aged 76, and was buried at Nhill.

Wheeling Matilda

Ted Ryko upon his return from Wildman River, Northern Territory in 1916

Though he was not as well known as Birtles or Mackay, Ted Ryko's contributions to the photographic documentation of aboriginal and outback life, botany and cycling history are enduring. Ryko's photographs and postcards are now collectors' items and nearly 200 still exist in Australian museums and libraries. A 375-specimen plant collection is now lodged at the State Herbarium in Adelaide and smaller ones exist in Melbourne, Sydney, Western Australia and the Northern Territory. The Darwin-Adelaide highway has now been pedalled in under five days, but no one is known to have broken his record over the old overlanders' route. His name is honoured in a Ted Ryko cycle track and Ryko Lookout in the Northern Territory.

5. The Humble Tool

By 1900 the novelty of the bicycle had worn off—'It creates no more interest (if as much) than the horse'—and in that year most of the cycle journals ceased publication. Attention increasingly focussed upon motor vehicles, the fastest means of personal transport and subject to an endless degree of modification, development, experimentation and consequent interest. The bicycle, however, did not become obsolete nor disappear from the scene.

The Orange, New South Wales insurance agent, nicknamed 'AMP' Carr (left) used the bicycle for many years. Doctor Cribb accompanied him on trips as far as Cobar and Condobolin to carry out physical examinations of life assurance applicants

Instead it was relegated to the status and role of a humble tool. The next two decades saw its greatest use throughout rural Australia, either from necessity or choice (by using bicycles two brothers who did stocktaking for goldfields mining firms netted more money from the shilling-per-mile travel allowance than from their salaries). It was adopted by many private and government organisations, and thousands of shearers, commercial travellers, workers, dentists, rouseabouts, prospectors, ministers of religion, tailors and boundary riders rolled silently about their business.

It was the heyday of rural cycling. If not spectacular, it was pervasive.

The Eastern Colonies

Unlike Western Australia, where there was a distinct, rapid, regional mass embrace of the bicycle as a rural tool, in the east there was a more gradual adoption by rural workers and travellers. Three months after Armstrong completed his overland ride of 1893 J.R. Brindle pedalled from Broken Hill to Sydney, and in 1894 C. Stewart rode from Melbourne to Brisbane. In Queensland there were several long rides over the next couple of years, including those of a politician who rode a thousand miles (1600 km) from Brisbane to Hughenden, Winton and Cloncurry, and a Brisbane insurance agent who, from January 1894 through July 1895, pedalled to the southwest of Queensland and adjacent parts of New South Wales, reaching as far as the Bulloo River and Coopers Creek. In 1896 a man and his wife cycled over 600 miles (1000 km) from Stainburn Downs (near Aramac) to Normanton in fifteen days.

By the mid-1890s bicycle shops and cycle clubs were found in many small towns. In the Wimmera a 'fair sprinkling of cyclists' was noted by mid-1896 and *The Australasian Pastoralists' Review* printed a letter from a station manager discussing the use of the bicycle on rural properties: '... their usefulness for station work seems to be overlooked by most owners and managers ... they can be ridden—and are ridden—across country. Even over loose, heavy ground ... A bicycle does not suffer from want of feed, so it does not matter how long it is kept ready to be mounted ... there are instances of long distances being ridden through bush. Only recently the bookkeeper at Wilgena, South Australia, rode on a bicycle from the station to Adelaide, 540 miles, and did the distance in four or five days, although much of the track is considered very heavy indeed … If any one in the bush does think of buying a bicycle, he should be careful to be thoroughly taught how to … repair it … even a big smash can be put in order by anyone with sense … I am quite sure it only needs for prejudice to be overcome to make the use of bicycles general for station work'. In inviting tenders for the construction of a fence around a paddock in 1897, one New South Wales property owner specified a cleared path for cycle-mounted riders.

The sudden focusing of attention upon cyclists in pastoral areas led a *Bulletin* cartoonist to suggest the eventual extinction of the horse, and E.S. Sorenson, in a typical *Bulletin* reaction to all cycling matters, to pen 'The Bicycle's Gone to the Bush' in mid-1897:

> It's all up the tree with the swagmen,
> It's all over now with the tramp,
> And the horsemen can dally with bagmen,
> For they're wanted no more on the camp.
> They're trooping in droves from the west-track,
> With tidings of woe to their push,
> For the inside, they say, is the best track,
> Since the bicycle's gone to the bush.
> On the stations out back they are riding
> 'Long Boundary and rabbit-proof fence;
> And rouseabouts swiftly are gliding
> With shearers and tank-seekers hence;
> They're rounding-up sheep and scrub-cattle,
> They stem the most desperate rush—
> E'en the Myalls will pedal to battle
> On the bikes that have gone to the bush.

The Shearers

By mid-1897 shearers were described as 'careering from station to station' on their bicycles and one had reportedly cycled nearly 2,000 miles (3,200 km) in the New South Wales interior. By 1900 the bicycle had been widely adopted by Australian shearers and was integral to their work migration pattern. In his book *On the Wool Track*, in 1909, C.E.W. Bean noted that as shearers came across New South Wales each year, the evidence of them was their bicycles which 'had spread through the country as fast as the rabbit'. As

Robert and Francis Lyon, from Tasmania, worked the New South Wales shearing circuit each year, covering several thousand miles between such places as Jerilderie, Narrandera, Yanco, Ivanhoe, Menindee, Wilcannia and Tibooburra

the shearing season got under way 'there began to appear—leaning against the huts around the big shearing-sheds of the "outside" Australia—bicycles ... it is extraordinary in what unlikely places one finds those tyre-tracks'. Bourke residents wrote of bicycles 'galore' being pedalled through the area and a wool classer working in western New South Wales from 1914–24 recalled sheds employing over a hundred men (including shed hands) in which nearly all rode bicycles. The use was so important that the Shed Hands' Agreement in New South Wales eventually required, in addition to food, bunk and other amenities, that 'the employer will provide a suitable room or other place, outside the kitchen and sleeping accommodation, for the housing of the ... cycles of the employees'.

In not requiring food, water or maintenance the bicycle was superbly suited to, and extended, the shearers' regime. They might work anywhere from a few days on a smaller property up to several weeks at a large sheep station—then have to travel sometimes great distances in often sparsely settled

Wheeling Matilda

An Australian Workers' Union Bicycle Corps at Coonamble, New South Wales in 1902, photographed by 'Banjo' Paterson

country to reach the next property. Shearers were extremely fit and when cutting out (completing work at a property) were capable of immediately pedalling off on a one-day trip of fifty miles (80 km) or more, if necessary. Two thousand miles (3,200 km) of travel would be routine during a season for many. In South Australia, for example, one group of shearers pedalled 550 miles (885 km) north along the Strzelecki Track to shear in southwest Queensland before returning to their home district for the local season. As well, the light, portable machine could easily be integrated with the rail network, where available. At wool sidings numerous shearers would 'climb down from the mail train and lift down their swags and their bicycles. As the train pulled out, they would already be stringing off through the white gate, the hubs and spokes of their machines twinkling across the paddock'.

The Western Australian Rabbit Fence

In 1859 a number of rabbits were imported into Victoria for sport hunting. While they provided some food both for people and working dogs, and their pelts extra income via the fur trade (used in the manufacture of the famous Akubra hat) their proliferation caused a rabbit plague that was

devastating to the environment. Extremely prolific and able to breed year-round in Australia's mild winters, this exotic species spread faster than any recorded mammal anywhere and their impact was immense. The rabbits destroyed vegetation, resulting in large scale erosion and the destruction of many native species of plants and animals. Farmers had to resort to fencing their paddocks to grow crops because shooting, ripping up the burrows and poisoning were ineffectual. Only with the release of the myxoma virus after 1950 were rabbits brought under relative control. However, increasing genetic resistance saw numbers increase to the point that another virus was released in the mid-1990s.

Originally confined to the eastern states, rabbits were migrating across the Nullarbor by 1900. In an effort to stem the westward migration and prevent them becoming established in the agricultural and pastoral areas of Western Australia, the government proposed a 2,035 mile (3,275 km) network of rabbit-proof fences that would be buried deep enough to prevent the rabbits from burrowing through, and high enough stop them leaping over. While perhaps delaying the spread, it was ultimately a forlorn effort. The animals came through when gates were left open, bushfires burned the fence posts, and feral camels and floods knocked over sections of the fence.

At a Royal Commission of Inquiry held in Perth in 1901 all witnesses

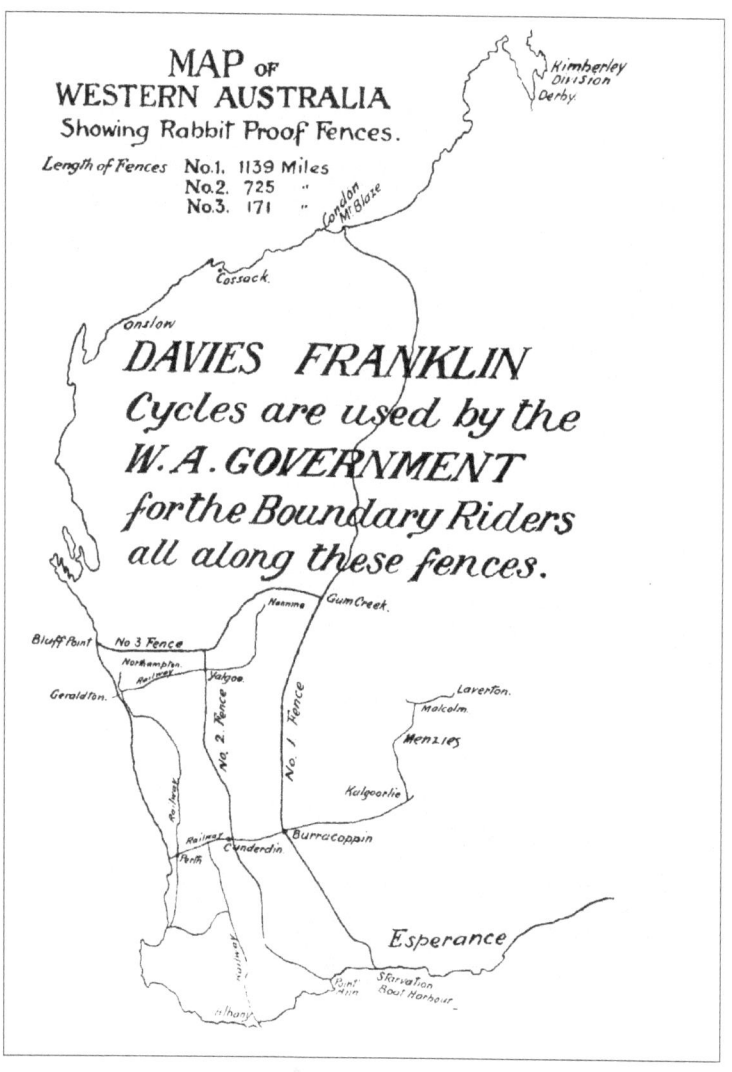

agreed that bicycles would be preferable to horses or camels to patrol the rabbit fence. In particular, bicycles cost much less than horses or camels to buy and maintain and the speed of cyclists would minimize the number of boundary riders needed, with consequent wage savings. Camel carts were used to transport supplies to depots along the line and to carry out repairs that could not be done by a cyclist alone, but a camel's willingness to eat poisonous plants resulted in the death of many and the need to constantly supervise their feeding habits was troublesome. Even after camel patrols were later introduced, bicycles continued to be relied upon in areas with a heavy concentration of poisonous plants. In particular, a lack of drinking water along the fence lines restricted the use of the animals (and any horses) for patrol and maintenance work.

A problem that plagued the Rabbit Department was illegal traffic along the fence. Permission was rarely granted for anyone to travel the fence reserve, because animals and vehicles tore holes in the wire and knocked down or bent the posts. Rough surfaces were created by cattle plodding along the fence, and vehicles drawn by horse or bullock. Some stretches were so cut up that cyclists could not patrol their assigned lengths in the period allowed, and two additional patrols had to be put on in 1908. In 1910 in the Barrambie area surreptitious wood carting traffic left the surface so rough that camel carts had to replace the cycle patrols completely. People illegally travelling the fence also took water from the tanks, a particular problem for bicycle-mounted riders because of the limited water supply they carried.

Bicycles were retired from the fence around 1915 after a majority of the staff volunteered to serve in the First World War, and patrol and maintenance logistics had to be radically reorganised. The camel cart was adopted for all riders, who now had both to patrol and undertake all maintenance work formerly done by separate repair crews. That was the only way they could carry posts, netting, food, water and other supplies. The bicycle, in these circumstances, was no longer a viable alternative.

Stewart Crawford used a bicycle during the 1930s as a rabbit inspector in the Western Australian wheat belt. He camped at a central location and spent two or three days cycling about adjacent properties, saving petrol, oil and maintenance expenses on his car. He could lift his bike over fences separating paddocks or neighbouring properties, and carry it across rough areas and watercourses that would have been impassable with a car, thus reducing duplicate travel. Seated on his machine he could have a close look without the nuisance of continually getting in and out of a car. The result was that he could cover more ground more thoroughly in a given area and inspect portions of properties which he might not otherwise have readily visited.

A rabbit fence patrol rider in 1908

Wheeling Matilda

Kalgoorlie Pipeline Lengthrunners

Ted Creasey (left and below), Kalgoorlie pipeline lengthrunner

The Kalgoorlie pipeline was completed in 1903 to supply water from the Mundaring Weir, near Perth, to the Eastern Goldfields, especially the towns of Coolgardie and Kalgoorlie. At 530 kilometres (330 miles) it was at the time the longest freshwater pipeline in the world. For the next six decades bicycles were used by 'lengthrunners' to patrol it. Each man rode a 15-mile (25 km) section roundtrip each day, keeping both the pipeline and the maintenance road alongside cleared of plant growth and notifying the office of any leaks or other problems. The high ratio of work to travel made the bicycle particularly effective in terms of cost and time and they were used until 1962.

Kangaroo Shooting and Timber Cutting

A classic example of the misperception of the potential for bicycle use in rural Australia is provided by the Melbourne *Cycling Times* of January 1896. The Australian writer reported that a London publication, *Pearson's Weekly*, had recently referred to the use of bicycles by kangaroo shooters, referring to the value of the 'noiseless approach' the machine afforded. The incredulous Melbourne writer informed his Australian readers that 'It is at once obvious that the [English] writer knows nothing about kangaroos, or the speed at which they [travel], nothing about Australian "country" and nothing about cycling'. In fact, that statement was most appropriate to the Australian writer himself. It is not known where the *Pearson's Weekly* information came from but it was true, for various kangaroo shooters used the bicycle.

Len Witt and Ernie Frandsen, cycling kangaroo shooters in Western Australia in the late 1920s and early 1930s, specifically referred to the value of the bicycle's quietness and the ability to cover extensive areas quickly while operating out of a central camp. Skins were carried back to camp on the rear carrier and handlebars.

Kangaroo shooter, Ernie Frandsen, at his camp on Dandaraga Station, Western Australia, circa 1930

In a similar vein, Herbert Barker had to supply logs for mine pit-props in Western Australia. The logs had to be relatively straight, seven feet long and at least four inches thick at the small end. Such trees were very widely scattered and the cutter could not find and cut enough in one day to keep Barker's camel team profitably occupied. Consequently Barker bought the cutter a bicycle, loaded it with water bags, axe, tucker and billy-can, and he was able to quickly cover a wider areas to cut trees, with Herbert following up to collect them.

The Decline of Rural Use

The gradual decline in cycling in rural Australia began about the end of the First World War and is related to the increasing availability, reliability, affordability and comfort of motor vehicles. For Australians the use of the motor vehicle was quickly and solidly established. In 1910 there were only about 5,000 in the country but by 1923 Australia ranked sixth in the world in terms of absolute numbers, with some 169,000 motor cars, commercial vehicles and motor cycles. In the next six years that number increased nearly fourfold and on a per capita basis Australian car ownership was exceeded only by the United States and New Zealand in 1930. An Englishman who

Fred Blakeley and his mates at Bloods Creek, South Australia on their way from Milparinka, New South Wales, to Darwin, circa 1908

visited Australia in 1928 commented upon the number of 'rough homes' that had motor cars parked outside.

As an identifiable group, shearers were among the first rural workers to abandon bicycles. Their work pattern—long periods at one location, punctuated by group travel to another point often established well ahead of time by contracts (they typically worked in teams)—put them in an excellent position to take advantage of shared motor transport costs. It made many shearers lose 'a good deal of their enthusiasm' for the bicycle.

However, there was a resurgence in the use of bicycles for rural work and travel during the harsh economic conditions of the 1930s Great Depression, with 'an invasion of bikes, with big bundles on the carriers or the rider's back, in pea-picking season and again at fruit-picking time'. As well, the bicycle still proved effective on occasion for boundary riding, mustering on stations and general rural work. At Nonning, South Australia, for example, during a severe drought men got 'heartily sick of using poor and knocked up horses' and used bicycles instead. They also mixed bicycles and motor cycles, using the latter for more distant work, and bicycles closer in and for droving (early motor cycles did not operate as well at extremely slow speeds as modern ones). And one stockman found that he could cycle his windmill circuit twice as fast as on a horse and spend the remaining time kangaroo shooting for extra money.

The severe restrictions on petrol and the limited availability of spare parts and tyres for motor vehicles during the Second World War contributed to the continued widespread rural use of the bicycle for several more years than would otherwise have been the case. The bicycle was long a popular device for commuting between urban and rural areas or between communities. In May 1925 a two-day traffic count along the Newcastle-Maitland Road tallied 5,511 bicycles and 2,573 motor cycles and cars. The extensive use of the bicycle for commuting in the area had been mentioned as early as 1903 by a mining inspector. Even into the 1950s substantial numbers of workers still commuted by bicycle about Australia; between Boulder and Kalgoorlie, to and from the smelter works at Port Pirie, and around the Collie area, with its numerous mines, for example. In the Townsville railway yards in Queensland, in 1980, there still existed 122 covered bicycle racks that were built in 1938, allocated by employee pay number, and fully used at least through the late 1940s. Another large covered shed, with yet more racks, was destroyed by Cyclone Althea in 1971.

A Human-Powered Strawberry Picker

Circa 1970, Jeff Bowcock of Tolga, Queensland designed and built a half dozen tricycles for both planting and harvesting strawberries. It cut down the time wasted in the large fields carrying pallets of strawberries to the ends of the long rows and returning with empty ones, and greatly decreased staff turnover.

The wheels run between the parallel rows of strawberries, the picker sitting in a comfortable seat of inner tube sections stretched between metal tubes suspended from the upper frame of the machine. The riders power the tricycles by pushing their feet against two independent levers or, for physical variety, moving the machine along by pulling against the ground with their feet. The front wheel can be locked into any of several positions but the machine essentially steers itself between the rows. The rider picks strawberries from either side with relatively little leaning, and full punnets are placed on pallets located over the rear axle. A cover over the machine protects both the rider and strawberries (which desiccate quickly in the heat once picked) from the direct sunlight, a great benefit to both; as one picker emphasised, she 'wouldn't be here if it weren't for it'.

Strawberry picker at Tolga, Queensland

Cycle-adapted machines in strawberry fields

Pedal Power

The potential of the bicyclist as a portable power source was quickly recognised. John Howard, mechanical manager of the Wolseley Sheep-Shearing Machine Company, invented an attachment for the bicycle that allowed the rear wheel to be raised off the floor, and a rubber wheel (with flywheel) lowered against the rotating bicycle wheel powered a hand-held shear. The flywheel doubled as a sharpening disc, and to increase the momentum it was recommended that the rear tyre be filled with water. The unit was demonstrated at the Sydney Show of the Royal Agricultural Society of New South Wales in 1899, reportedly enabling a sheep to be shorn in four to five minutes. It was suggested that the machine could be used for cream separation and rotary brushing as well. The *Australian Pastoralists' Review* thought that 'as the bicycle is fast growing in favour with shearers in search of employment, it is only reasonable to suppose that they will have the patent shearing process gear attached to their bicycles'. It is not known how many of the machines were manufactured nor how successfully or extensively they were used. I suspect that a major factor inhibiting their widespread use was that it required one man to pedal and another to shear.

Alfred Traegar with his pedal wireless

Property owners probably felt that instead they would be better off simply having both men use blade shears.

In World War I bicycles were used to power electrical generators and in Australia Alfred Traegar subsequently developed a generating device that came to be known as the pedal wireless, although it was actually a pedal-powered generator that produced electricity for a separate wireless receiver. In conjunction with Reverend John Flynn, who ran the Australian Inland Mission, they eventually launched in 1928 what would come to be known as the Royal Flying Doctor Service, using aircraft provided by Hudson Fysh, founder of Qantas. The pedal wireless was quickly adopted on a large scale and revolutionised outback communications, enabling widespread provision of services to remote areas by councils, medical workers, and others. As well, it allowed direct vocal communication between teachers and isolated distance education students through the School of the Air, launched in Alice Springs in June 1951. Later schools followed in Western Australia, New South Wales and Queensland.

The Tyres

The durability and reliability of the pneumatic tyre were ultimately the keys to the widespread rural use of the bicycle. Riders typically used 1¼-inch (32 mm) wide roadster tyres and one of the most impressive facts to come out of the research is the serviceability and high quality of tyres in those days. Numerous long journeys were reportedly made with few or no punctures, and correspondence, interviews and the general tone of the literature suggest that such accomplishments were not exaggerated. The *W.A. Wheelman* judged the Dunlops so good by 1898 that 'cyclists have almost forgotten that dread fear of puncturing that existed a few seasons back'.

Given the number of thorny plants around, many bush cyclists also used thorn proof tyres, the most popular by far being the Dunlop Thorn Proof. It had twice the roadster tyre's fabric thickness and a fifty per cent thicker rubber tread. Though heavier to pedal, former bush cyclists said that it was not substantially so. Interestingly, some suggested that the difference was hardly noticeable in paddocks and other off-road and soft riding conditions, where the twenty per cent greater tread width of 1½ inches (38 mm) allowed easier rolling over soft surfaces than the narrower tyres, and hence compensated for the otherwise greater rolling resistance. The Dunlop tyre was widely used and proved to be highly effective, a point frequently cited during personal interviews, in the literature, and (not unexpectedly) in Dunlop advertisements.

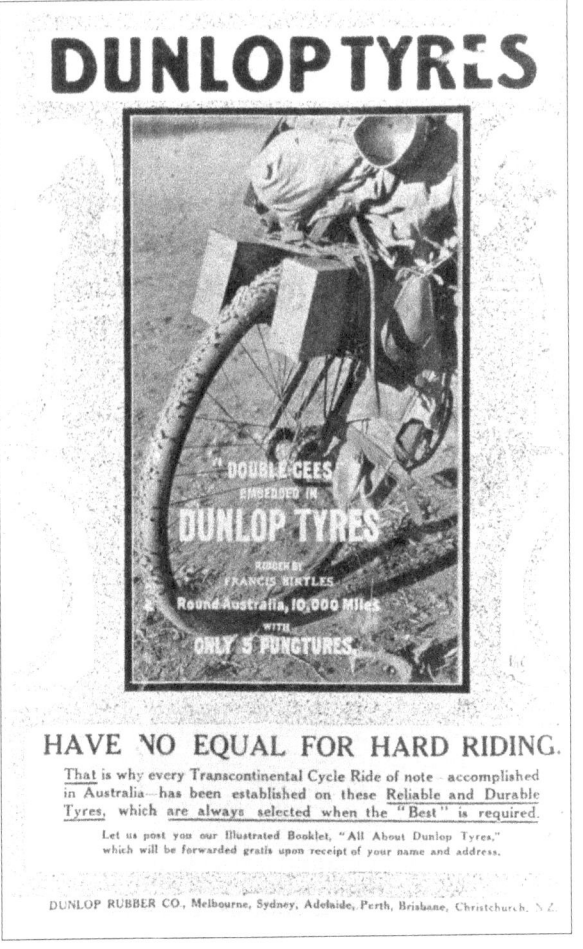
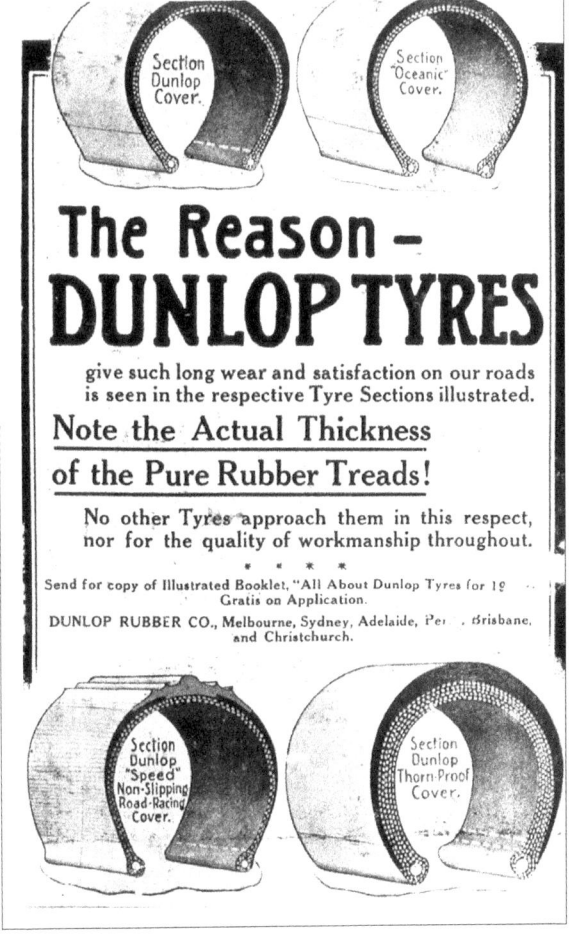

Dunlop tyre advertisements

The Bicycle at War

The fact that Australian soldiers have used bicycles in wartime comes as a surprise to many. However, of the four most significant military uses of the bicycle—in the Boer War, World War I, the Japanese invasion of Malaya, and Vietnam—ANZACs were the only forces officially represented in all of them. The key concept is that of 'bicycling' which, as emphasised at the opening of the book, involves using bicycles but not necessarily riding them. Many military minds over the years never came to grips with that fact. Others did and adopted them to great effect against their enemies.

The Boer War

The bicycle was first wheeled into the military spotlight in South Africa, from 1899-1902. Australian cyclists along with several thousand British soldiers, scouts, Boer commandos, and messengers found the machine to be highly effective. They pushed, pedalled and carried their bicycles over the high veldt and across the sand and salt pans of the eastern Kalahari Desert, not unlike much of Australia's landscape. Bicycling technology was also adapted to laying telecommunications lines, for wheeled stretchers, and patrolling railway lines with specialised war cycles.

The Boers (mostly Dutch Calvinists) settled the Cape Province in 1652. In 1806 the British annexed the Cape Colony but their subsequent relations with the Boers were uneasy. In 1835-37 the Boers marched inland to establish their own new colonies, the Orange Free State and Transvaal. Following the discovery of diamonds and gold on Boer lands in the late 1800s pressure was put upon the British government to annex those colonies as well. By December 1896 tensions were high and powerful mining interests attempted to initiate a rebellion against the Boer government, led by Dr. Leander S. Jameson.

Jameson's force of some 600 men, mostly Rhodesian police, marched towards Johannesburg to encourage British residents and other foreigners to rise up against the Boer government. The raid was a fiasco but while Jameson's horse column trod slowly across the landscape, express cycle riders, in contrast, 'scoured the country at will' at the rate of fifteen miles (24 km) an hour, carrying messages between his column and Johannesburg. One rider was intercepted by Boers but they did not discover the dispatch he had concealed in the saddle pillar. The machine's manufacturer, Osmond Cycles, ran worldwide advertisements showing the dispatch rider pointing to the hidden missive. The exploits of the cycle dispatch riders were reported at great length, within days, in various local and overseas newspapers, magazines and cycle journals. The net effect was to widely publicise the speed of the machine and its military potential on the South African veldt.

Some 20,000 Australians served in South Africa and the British Commander, Lord Roberts, noted that they and other colonial volunteers could find their way about the countryside better than the British. 'No other troops had lived under conditions so similar to those of the Boers, or knew better a country of such wide distances'. As Western Australians had more experience than anyone else in the world at that time in using bicycles over expansive, arid areas, they had strong views about the potential effectiveness of their bush cyclists: 'From England, wheelmen are being sent out attached to several corps, but to Australians it is somewhat amusing to read that their machines are of the heavy roadster type, and are fitted with mudguards and brakes. A hundred of such cyclists would not be as valuable as half a dozen of the pioneer wheelmen of Australia'.

Photograph of dispatch rider used in the Osmond Cycle advertisement

This sentiment was echoed by Percy Armstrong, Western Australia's largest cycle dealer, who added this tactical point for consideration: 'A low set, swiftly moving cyclist, swinging along the winding track, would be a more difficult object to aim at than the horseman. Also dozens of bullets might pass through the machine without touching it or at least without doing much damage, whereas one bullet through a horse would very soon stop the rider's career'. For the benefit of the paper's readers Armstrong reported that the Boers commandeered 'all the good makes of bicycles' in Johannesburg, specifically Humbers, for which he was the Perth dealer.

Many of the Australian cyclists who served in the war joined units which officially required every member to be an expert horseman. However, cyclists were recruited in some units out of respect for their proven knowledge of bush lore and ability to travel rapidly through the outback. The Queensland Imperial Bushmen's unit, for example, included a cyclist company of fifty-one men mounted on Massey-Harris bicycles furnished by the government. Among Australian cyclists was Arthur Richardson, who had recently made the first solo ride around the Australian continent in 1899-1900.

Herbert Plumer, who had served in the Sudan and would later command the British Second Army in World War I, commanded forces which included a Cyclist Corps of six officers and 79 men. His troops consisted of 'colonial irregulars' from the British South Africa Police, South Rhodesian Volunteers, and the misnamed Rhodesian Regiment, made up heavily of Canadians and Australians. Plumer initially defended Rhodesia against Boer incursions across the Limpopo River but soon took the war to them by pushing south along the rugged Transvaal-Bechuanaland border. In that arid countryside with its sandy surfaces and salt pans he established forward camps and maintained a cycle communication network. One of his Australian officers, Lieutenant Wynyard Joss, wrote a personal account of an incident in which twenty of his cycle mounted troops fought a group of Boers, killing and capturing several. 'We have paralysed the English officers

Australian and Canadian volunteers with the Rhodesian Regiment

The Story of Australian Cycling

This machine was adapted for quickly unreeling and taking up telegraph wires

at the way we ride over the rocks and ruts here ... if you saw the country we travelled over you would say we were mad to attempt it on bicycles'.

By early 1901 the British developed a strategic policy based upon a series of fortified blockhouses they had built to protect the railway lines from Boer raids. The blockhouses were basic cylindrical corrugated iron water tanks of differing diameters placed one inside another, the interstices filled with rock, small portholes cut, and a roof added. It was cheap and effective. Each blockhouse was staffed by a handful of men and within sight of the next, with overlapping fields of fire. Strands of barbed wire were strung along the railway lines between them, together with trip wire signals and trenches to prevent wagons crossing. The blockhouses were linked by telephone and telegraph and the railway lines patrolled by armoured trains. The result was a network of blockhouse-and-wire barriers crisscrossing the countryside, which was extremely difficult for mounted Boers to traverse.

Fortified blockhouse

Ultimately the network was extended to encompass roads and the open veldt. By the end of the war there were over eight thousand blockhouses interspersed along 3,700 miles (4,350 km) of corridors. The original railway defensive network was thus converted to an offensive system and the British forces undertook systematic 'drives' across each of the countryside's wired

Two-man railway cycle

Cape Town railway yard

off compartments. Eventually 'there came a day when there was nowhere left to go, and no Boers free to go there'.

The most interesting use of bicycle technology in the Boer War was the creation of 'war cycles' to patrol the railway lines, constructed by Donald Menzies in Cape Town. The two-man version weighed sixty pounds (24 kg) and could achieve a speed of thirty miles (48 km) per hour, but only for a short distance. It was relatively easy to pedal along railway grades, ran 'all but noiselessly,' and could carry two passengers and a Maxim gun. Painted khaki, it was 'difficult to see even at comparatively short distances' and was light enough to be lifted from the line. Because it did not need steering the riders were free to shoot and observe from the smooth riding platform. With its fixed wheel it could also be pedalled forward or backward. At least a score of the two-man war cycles had been constructed by mid-1901.

The Military Relay Rides

After the Boer War Australia's military authorities were pressured to develop bicycle-mounted troop units, as many nations were doing abroad, but refused to do so. The greatest lobbying was by Dunlop, which sponsored (sometimes covertly) a series of relay rides to demonstrate the value of the bicycle for military dispatch work. The financial benefits accruing would be great, given Dunlop's near monopoly of the Australian tyre market. A relay ride from Melbourne to Colac and back was planned as early as 1893 'to show the public what really can be accomplished on the safety' but was cancelled because of unsuitable weather and upcoming cycle races preempting riders' interest.

The first major relay ride, in Western Australia, in 1899, was arranged by Alf Mather, the local Dunlop representative (and former Darwin-Adelaide overlander), to demonstrate the speed with which cyclists could carry a dispatch 250 miles (400 km) between Albany and Perth in the event of a 'foreign invasion interfering with our telegraph and railway service'. Mather calculated that the run could be made in about fifteen hours using a relay of riders. The ride started in rain at 12.30 am Saturday morning at Albany, and was scheduled to arrive at 3.30 that afternoon in Perth. Extremely heavy rains and several cyclists not being ready at their posts meant a handful of riders had to do the whole route, one riding five legs. The last rider rode to the Perth Police Station for a time stamp at 1.37 am, in lieu of waking up His Excellency, to whom he was originally instructed to deliver the message. Perhaps it was as well that Sir Gerard had not been present for the rider would have had nothing to hand him: the dispatch itself was lost on the Kojonup sand patch, a fact quietly buried in a brief report some one and a half weeks later. The ride was anything but a success and a second attempt a few weeks later was cancelled because of influenza. Mather probably wished the whole episode had never been dreamt up.

Although not officially sponsored by Dunlop, the fact that their agent had been the organizer, and that it had failed in its objective led to the firm taking a cautionary attitude towards such future events. They had much to gain if successful, of course, but if the events failed they could hinder the selling of bicycles and tyres to the military. The first officially sanctioned Dunlop relay ride was not to take place for another ten years.

By 1909 Dunlop had proposed the idea of a Dispatch Relay Ride between Adelaide and Sydney, via Melbourne. The 1,143 miles (1,839 km) were to be ridden in eighty hours by sixty-four relay teams of two men each, to demonstrate the dependability of the bicycle under a variety of conditions of weather and terrain. It was known as the Dunlop Military Dispatch Cycle Ride after the Chief of the General Staff formally endorsed the idea (it cost the military nothing to do so). In exchange the military requested a report on the ride and copies of a map of the Coorong area that Dunlop had prepared especially for the trip, the most detailed yet compiled. As military endorsement imparted an aura of national importance to the venture, Dunlop took advantage of this in its publicity.

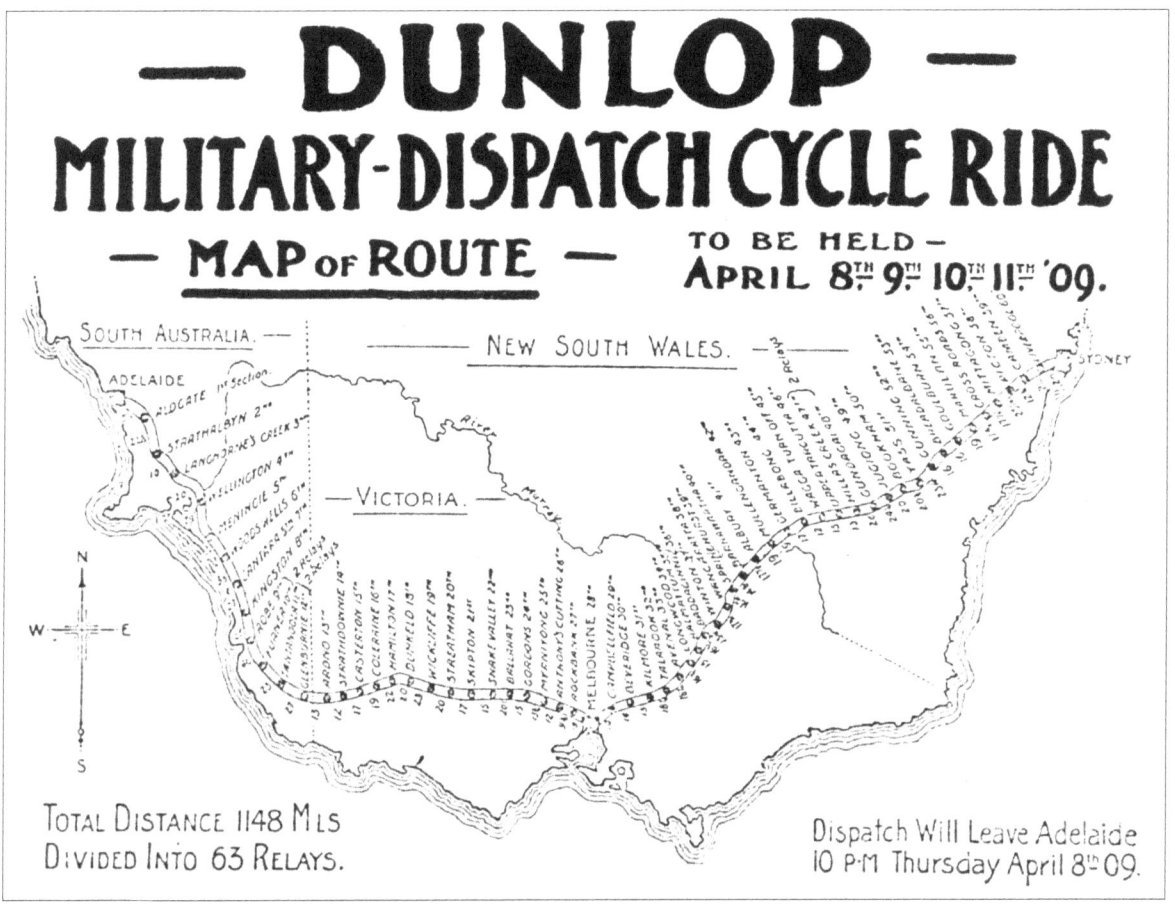

The route of the 1909 and 1912 Dunlop Military-Dispatch Cycle Rides

In preparation for the trip a Dunlop team motored over the route, interviewed riders, investigated conditions, and affixed red discs to trees, posts and fences at the changing stations. The greatest concern was the Coorong area, where sand dunes and flats, marshy lagoon edges, and backwater reaches represented a 'horrible stretch of country'. The departure from Adelaide was timed to allow it to be ridden in daylight. The ride was divided into sixty-four stages, each ridden by two riders so in case of a breakdown the remaining rider could continue. The final time allotted for the ride was 73½ hours.

By the time the riders reached Melbourne they were so far ahead of schedule that later dispatch riders might not be waiting for them. Telegrams were sent to all riders further along the route. Though it was night and many of them lived on farms or away from the nearest telegraph offices, there were no serious delays. There were numerous accidents along the way. One rider crashed into a creek and another collided with a flock of sheep at night, several experienced falls, and there were some punctures, but the dispatch was handed over in Sydney 69 hours and 35 minutes after having left Adelaide. It was a highly successful effort, four hours ahead of schedule and some ten hours faster than felt possible when the relay was first conceived. But the military still did not create cyclist units.

By mid-1911 the speed and reliability of motor cycles and motor cars during various overland journeys led to suggestions that they could negotiate the 1909 military dispatch route far quicker than cyclists. This led Dunlop to plan a second relay ride matching cyclists against motor cyclists and motor cars. Again the military endorsed it in exchange for a detailed report on the ride. The 1912 ride was highly publicised with the bicycle, whose reliability and speed was known, pitted against the more fascinating, less common, less reliable, but faster motor vehicles. The *Daily Telegraph* called it 'the greatest sporting event ever promoted in Australia, if not the whole world', one that would be watched by 'some millions of interested people'.

The 1912 relay race was run over the same route as the 1909 ride. An extra team of cyclists was added, but otherwise the race conditions remained essentially the same as before. The motor cars ran only four

Two pairs of a South Australian relay team

legs: Adelaide–Mount Gambier–Melbourne–Albury–Sydney, while fifty-two motor cyclists rode twenty-six legs.

Harry James, Dunlop's organiser, allowed the cyclists to start thirty hours ahead of the motor cars and twenty-four hours ahead of the motor cycles. Newspapers suggested that the motor cyclists would easily win the race, but critics pointed out that during some of the night stretches the motor cycles (as well as cars) would not be able to exceed the cyclists' speed, and while the motor vehicles were capable of forty miles (64 km) per hour on good roads, such stretches were 'few and far between on the overland route from Adelaide to Sydney'. The 'absolute reliability' of the bicycles was considered an important factor.

The race began on Good Friday, 5 April 1912, at 5 am and the cyclists faced an ominous situation. It was raining, strong headwinds were blowing, and the roads as far as Melbourne were already reported heavy. By 5 am Saturday, when the motor cyclists left, rain was still coming down. When the motor cars departed at 11 am the weather was clearing. The roads, however, were very heavy and rain was again encountered to the south; no one was able to take advantage of the moonlight during the race.

The cyclists pedalled a remarkable ride. Although they suffered from rain, wind and muddy roads most of the way, they succeeded in bettering the 1909 time by three minutes with few problems. In contrast, one motor cyclist broke his leg (his partner fell twice in the same stretch), another broke a hand, and a third bruised a shoulder. One's engine seized and his partner broke his motorcycle's frame. In descending Jugiong Mount two motor cyclists hit a fence, and the next pair had one's rear tyre blow out, while his partner was delayed with a wet magneto. In the early stages the motor cyclists had a difficult time closing the gap on the cyclists; they covered one 36-mile (58 km) Coorong stretch only one minute faster than the cyclists. The motor cyclists eventually drew closer to the cyclists, but were unable to catch them. They arrived in Sydney six hours and eighteen minutes after the cyclists.

The motor cars started out well, and the run over the Coorong was among the fastest legs of the entire journey. The wet sand offered a firm surface and the driver averaged 35 miles (56 km) per hour on the sandy stretch, far faster than anyone thought possible. While the cars suffered no notable mechanical troubles, rain and slippery roads eventually slowed the pace considerably. One car got lost for a while in western Victoria and had three punctures before reaching Melbourne, the drivers a 'sorry spectacle'. On the last leg the car with the dispatch took a wrong turnoff, arriving in Sydney an hour after his partner had, some eight hours after the cyclists, and two hours after the motor cyclists.

For the 1912 race a military report was filed by two officers. The motor cars had covered the distance in 46 hours 44 minutes; the motor cyclists in 51 hours 50 minutes; and the cyclists in 69 hours 32 minutes. They judged the bicycle, although slower, more reliable than either of the other vehicles and less likely to be put out of action by road and weather conditions or either mechanical or tyre troubles. However, they felt that the bad roads had not allowed either the cars or motor cycles to demonstrate their best work. And despite the fact that the cars proved faster on the trip they inexplicably deemed the motor cycles, plagued by rider and mechanical problems, superior to bicycles and cars for the transmission of messages. The tone of the report conveys the impression that they had already decided that motor cycles were best, then proceeded to qualify the race conditions and results to justify that prejudice. Their final conclusion was that it would be difficult, if not impossible, to organise such a ride in wartime since it required several weeks of organisation and depended upon the very postal and telegraph facilities they were intended to replace. Though the cyclists' performance was impressive, the military refused to sanction any large cycle units, feeling cyclists were best employed individually or as small groups attached to other units.

World War I

When the Great War started in August 1914 the British, for example, had some 14,000 men in formal cyclist regiments and battalions and by war's end there were over 20,000. That did not include an unknown but much larger number of cyclists attached to virtually every British military unit (including cavalry) as messengers, orderlies and couriers. From early 1916 a reorganisation resulted in each corps having several cyclist companies totalling 500 men. It was calculated that at least 100,000 British soldiers and 150,000 French and Belgians used bicycles in some capacity. Even the American Expeditionary Forces took 29,000 bicycles with them when they sailed to Europe in 1917.

At the outbreak of war cyclist soldiers demonstrated their great mobility and value. On the fluid battlefields during the first weeks of fighting cyclists were everywhere, with newspaper articles and personal accounts relating the exploits of cycling soldiers riding ahead of all other forces, taking important positions, bridges, and roads. They variously rode down and captured the enemy, saved their comrades' lives, and pedalled through hostile fire to deliver messages and warnings.

The bicycle's major advantages were highlighted. The quiet machines could move quickly along roads crowded with wagons, cars, large numbers of marching troops, and fleeing civilians. Soldiers readily pedalled 50 to 100 miles (80 to 160 km) per day, and night rides of 50 miles (80 km) were common. Prone soldiers, with their bicycles lying alongside, were relatively inconspicuous in the trees, foliage and grass. Horse drawn German ammunition wagons 'had no chance of escape from cyclists' and were captured and destroyed by them, a fact pointedly noted in a 1925 German Army analysis of wartime cycle use. A British soldier found that 'the push-bike could be made to go almost anywhere and at a speed which left infantryman far behind'. Belgian cavalry officer Lt. Raoul Daufresne admitted that the bicycle was much quicker than horses, no small concession from a man who had been complimented by the King of England for his London show riding.

However, as millions of men and vast amounts of materiel from each side converged to do battle on a scale never before seen, the internal combustion engine, machine gun and artillery quickly altered the nature and dimensions of the war. Both armies sought protection by digging thousands of miles of interconnecting zigzag trenches and stringing barbed wire between opposing lines, sometimes only a few yards apart. The internal combustion engine played an increasingly critical role. The British Expeditionary Force, for example, took only 842 motorised vehicles to France in August 1914, 90 per cent of those requisitioned. Four years later the British alone were using some 113,000 cars, trucks, motor cycles and motorised bicycles. Overhead, the airplane came of age and assumed tactical and strategic importance. By the end of the war more than 200,000 had been built and the Germans were bombing London from the Continent. Ultimately, a new technology—the tank—helped to break the stalemate that the trench-based war became.

Nonetheless the bicycle remained extremely valuable. While trench warfare was not conducive to cycle charges, cyclists served everywhere behind the lines for delivering messages, moving troops, directing traffic, and generating electrical power. However, cyclist soldiers were routinely reassigned to depleted infantry units to serve in the firing line and many cycle units were effectively disbanded or operated at limited levels. That was the case with the London Cyclist Battalion, the most famous in the world. Through late 1915 they rode coastal patrols in the south of England, watching out for a possible German invasion and fighting fires set by raiding German aircraft. When they finally shipped abroad to India, in December 1915, they went as infantrymen, without bicycles. 'It was a bitter blow' wrote one battalion member.

The ANZAC Cyclist Battalions

The life of cyclist soldiers during the Great War is well illustrated by the ANZAC (Australian and New Zealand Army Corps) Cyclist Battalions. The 1st ANZAC Cyclist Battalion was comprised solely of Australians; the 2nd ANZAC Cyclist Battalion (widely known as the NZ Cyclist Battalion) was

A cycle battalion, including ANZACS and Canadians, parading before Lord French in Europe

a Kiwi unit. The two battalions spent the war moving frequently from one billet to another along the Western Front, the New Zealanders living in 82 different locations. Many soldiers were temporarily reassigned and at any given time either battalion might be half-depleted. Those remaining were engaged in such tasks as directing traffic, unloading railway goods wagons, felling trees, burying cables in no man's land (a New Zealand specialty), harvesting hops for local families, repairing trenches and burying the dead.

However unheralded, the ANZAC cyclists carried their share of the war burden. Of the 708 men who served in the Kiwi battalion at one time or another, 59 were killed and 259 wounded. They took home 72 British, French and Belgian medals. The Australian battalion worked a much greater portion of its time behind the lines in traffic control and other functions and only 13 members were killed; the number killed or wounded while serving with other units, though, is unknown. Of the 295,000 Australians who served in France, twenty per cent died and another 52 per cent were casualties.

The Commander of the Australian Battalion was Jacob Edwin Hindhaugh, from the western district of Victoria. He went to Gallipoli in

Major Jack Hindaugh (right), commander of the 1st ANZAC Cyclist battalion

1915, was wounded and evacuated to Egypt. He served there as aide-de-camp to Colonel (later Lt.-General Sir Harry) Chauvel, Commander of the Desert Mounted Corps. Hindhaugh was a noted horseman, excellent speaker, socially confident, ruggedly handsome and physically tough. Known as Gentleman Jockey Jack, he broke in mounts for other officers, conducted riding tests, played polo, rode in races in Cairo and entertained visiting dignitaries and their wives.

When the ANZAC forces were restructured Captain Hindhaugh was offered a camel squadron but turned it down: 'camels stank'. He was subsequently given the command of a Cyclist Corps. He made no comment at the time in his personal diary as to his reaction, but two months later, after General Birdwood had inspected his troops, Hindhaugh wrote that 'Birdie asked me if I had come down to riding cycles and could I ride them as well as I can a horse'.

Why the ANZAC Cyclist Battalions were formed is not entirely clear. During the previous two decades Australia's military authorities had refused to sanction independent cyclist units and the fighting conditions on the Western Front were quite clearly defined by early 1916. The Chief of the General Staff, Colonel (later Maj.-General Sir William) Bridges had long argued that cyclists were best employed individually or in small groups as messengers for larger units. Most likely the Cyclist Corps came about because the Australians based their new divisional structure upon the British pattern, which included cyclist units. Generals White and Birdwood, who expanded the ANZAC divisions from three to six in only a few weeks, had little time for reflection—if the British were doing it, it was probably good enough for the moment.

Captain Hindhaugh had even less time to prepare his men. He was advised of his command on 14 March and nine days later shipped out to Europe. In that time he had to create, fit out and train the unit and the problems were legion. The commanding officer of another cyclist company, for example, found that 'a number of the men had never ridden a bicycle previously, and a good deal of time was wasted in teaching them'. Also they could not all use firearms, 'many of the men transferred not having the slightest idea'. Some were firing service rifles for the first time and a 'big percentage of the men were "gun shy". Unfortunately, the short time available did not permit this tendency to be corrected'. Puncture kits, accessories and spare parts were in short supply and non-military bicycles were pressed into service. Even so, some men still did not have machines by embarkation.

The New Zealand Cyclist Company, in contrast, was formed in New Zealand, had two months to recruit men (principally from the Mounted Rifles), and made sure they could pedal and shoot. In the southern hemisphere autumn of May 1916 the unit sailed for Europe with 204 men and 206 bicycles. After 46 days of travel they arrived in Egypt suffering from seasickness and the terrific heat of the Gulf of Suez. Soon afterward they left for France.

On 23 March Hindhaugh's men boarded the SS Briton for Marseille and the Mediterranean crossing left many of the men sick. Upon disembarkation they immediately entrained for the Western Front, trading the heat of Egypt for a bivouac in the midst of a late northern European winter; it was cold and rained and snowed virtually continuously throughout April. Within days men were falling ill and being evacuated, the start of two and a half years of illness, disease, death and boredom for Hindhaugh's unit.

Diphtheria and meningitis epidemics forced an isolation of the battalion at one stage, scabies and trench fever required the blankets to be fumigated, influenza swept the battalion, and foot problems were endemic. Within two months of arrival in Europe Major Hindhaugh was afflicted with severe attacks of hay fever which plagued him throughout his service.

Coming from relatively sunny climes the Aussies found the cold winters hard to take. They discovered that riding bicycles through deep snow, a new experience, was impossible and pushing the heavily laden machines up snow-covered and icy slopes was taxing—'spills were frequent and our tempers sullen'. The colonials were not alone in their despair. An Englishman in Flanders found that 'a whole winter in this war-stricken country, with its atrocious roads and impossible by-ways is enough to dispel any ideas [about the joy] of riding'.

Eventually Hindhaugh was placed in charge of the 1st ANZAC Cyclist Battalion. To celebrate the appointment and new rank, that night he went into the Officer's Club in the nearby town of Poperinghe with his mates. They had 'a good time. McDougal had a few falls off his bike in consequence on the way home'.

Although the battalion never served in the front trenches as a unit, it was subjected to regular bombardment from artillery and airplanes and one man was 'blown to pieces' while in his dugout. His men had to bury the dead which, on one occasion, had 'been laying out for two or three weeks'. The New Zealand cyclist troops were eventually used to lay cables between front line trenches and the primary and subsidiary support trenches. It involved digging ditches some two metres (6½ feet) deep, standing sometimes waist-deep in water, and normally done at night without lights to avoid the enemy pinpointing the workers and calling artillery down upon them. They proved so adept that most were eventually assigned to supervisory roles.

The combat, monotony and dragging on of the war took their toll on morale. By early 1917 Australian soldiers found that 'the buoyancy of even a year earlier was now foreign to them'. Major Hindhaugh was no exception. He was 'sick up of everything—dam [sic] the war'. Once, when all troops in the area but his were moved out, he commented that 'the village is very quiet. We are left in a backwash—hope they forget us altogether'. Two weeks later he had a look at the results of the fighting in the trenches: there were 'dead everywhere. Awful sight'.

In October 1918 Major Hindhaugh left for a furlough in Australia. It is not clear whether he was to return to Europe if the war continued. It did not, and he did not. He received a personal note from General Birdwood and wore his greatcoat and spurs at his farewell speech to the battalion. His diary suggests no regret at leaving. Like so many others, Major Hindhaugh was 'fed up', 'sick up', 'and 'tired' of it all. He was one of the lucky ones to see home again, and died in Victoria in 1959.

Early the following year the 1st ANZAC Cyclist Battalion was disbanded and consigned to history. Among its last official acts, some of the men paraded before the King on Salisbury Plain, in England. As the Australians pushed their machines past him a few were caught on motion picture film for a few seconds. The routinely under-strength Australian battalion got scant reference in the *Official History* of the war, and virtually no mention in any other book. The Kiwis were slightly better known, principally as a result of a *Regimental History* the officers produced in 1922.

The Invasion of Malaya-Singapore

The bicycle's most effective and widely publicised use by infantry took place in hot, tropical Malaya. In November 1939 Winston Churchill emphasized to his cabinet colleagues that Singapore was a fortress that could only be taken by a siege of fifty thousand men. Such an effort was adjudged forlorn and subject to interruption at will by superior British naval forces. He did not consider it possible that the Japanese would embark on such a mad enterprise.

They did. In December 1941, one and a half hours before the attack upon Pearl Harbor, Japanese troops began landing in northeast Malaya. Seventy days later Singapore fell to a force of only 35,000 Japanese soldiers. It was the most intensive and significant use of cycle-mounted fighting troops in military history. The device, given little consideration by British military planners since World War I, gave the Japanese an immense advantage in tactical mobility on the Malayan Peninsula. It was the time 'when Tojo came a-wheeling'. Many simply could not believe it. Others could not believe it could be so simple. They pedalled into military legend, stunning their Australian and other British Empire enemies with the speed of their advance and ability to carry out rapid flanking manoeuvres.

In lieu of the horse transport Japanese troops had used in China,

Wheeling Matilda

Masanobu Tsuji, who planned the attack, reorganised each regiment so that all heavy materials could be loaded onto about fifty trucks. Officers and men not riding the trucks used bicycles. Churchill later accused Tsuji, who had reconnoitred the peninsula ahead of time, of having stored large numbers of bicycles in Malaya. However, Japan had been exporting cheap bicycles to the country for years and Tsuji said that the machines were so ubiquitous that his men simply picked them up in local towns, villages and rubber plantation settlements. Ultimately each division ended up with some five hundred motor vehicles and six thousand bicycles. Each cyclist

Japanese cyclists entering Singapore

carried upwards of sixty-five pounds (30 kg) on his machine as well as a light machine gun or rifle. F. Spencer Chapman, a British soldier who remained behind the lines as a guerrilla fighter throughout the war, described their advance as consisting of 'waves of cyclists and motor transport'. The majority rode in groups of forty or fifty, three or four abreast, 'talking and laughing just as if they were going to a football match'. They travelled lightly and were equipped with a motley assortment of gear. The only standard equipment he observed was a mackintosh cape with hood that covered the rider and paraphernalia; with 'extraordinary determination' they pedalled right through the tropical downpours.

Tsuji's essential tactic was to rely not upon traditional artillery bombardments preceding the troops, but upon lightly armed troops moving quickly ahead of their tank support. The bicycles were integral to the tactics. One advantage lay in the relative ease and rapidity with which cyclist troops could overcome various obstacles. At blown bridgeheads temporarily impassable to motor vehicles, troops could wade bicycles across shallow streams, carry them over lightweight makeshift bridges (some no more than logs supported on the shoulders of colleagues), or ferry them across in small boats. In that way continual pressure was kept upon retreating British forces. In particular, Japanese cyclists utilised the rubber estates' well developed network of plantation roads and narrow paths for rapid encircling manoeuvres to surprise British troops from behind. Tsuji's summary of the situation was that 'thanks to Britain's dear money spent on the excellent paved roads, and to the cheap Japanese bicycles, the assault on Malaya was easy'.

The cycle columns rolling southward down the west coast sometimes got into trouble because of the very rapidity of movement—as illustrated in an ambush set up by Australians at a crossing of the Gemencheh River on 14 January 1942.

A company of the 2/30th Battalion went three miles up the road beyond the bridge, toward the Japanese advance, and hid. In the late afternoon some three hundred Japanese cyclists rode past the ambush position; after an interval another eight hundred or so followed. The 'blithely chattering Japanese push cyclists, riding five or six abreast ... resembled a picnic party rather than part of an advancing army, except that they carried arms'. The

Masanobu Tsuji

Australians then blew the bridge and sprang the trap on the completely surprised Japanese, who took some time to go into action as their 'rifles and automatic guns were strapped to their cycles'. The invading forces suffered nearly a thousand casualties. The Australian ambush, one of the few successful momentary hindrances to the Japanese advance, was eventually broken up by advancing support tanks.

The Japanese use of the bicycle in Malaya is so widely known that it has almost become a cliché in summarising that campaign. But the machine was also widely employed by Japanese troops in other theatres of operation. An Australian writer in *The Bulletin*, commenting upon an advance in Burma in February 1942, described the Japanese movement beyond a damaged bridgehead as 'their usual dribble of manpower, which flowed on—on bicycle, on foot'. In New Guinea, some thirty miles inland and three thousand feet up from coastal Buna, 'the Japanese were seen coming down the road to Awala. They wore green uniforms and steel helmets garnished with leaves. Some were on bicycles. Each carried in addition to his arms and ammunition a machete for cutting through the jungle, a mess tin of cooked rice, and a shovel slung on his back'. They did not stop there. A photograph in the Australian War Memorial shows a bicycle found along the notorious Kokoda Trail. It is a wonder anyone could have got it that far.

An Australian soldier with an abandoned Japanese bicycle on the Kokoda Trail

The Australian Home Front

World War II, with its unprecedented and nearly insatiable military demand for fuel, tyres, vehicles and parts, left civilian public and private transport in dire straits on many home fronts and in utter chaos in others. Private motorised travel ceased for a substantial percentage of the world's population for the duration of the war. In many European countries cycling had long been an integral element of the local transport scene and wartime domestic reliance upon it represented little change for much of the population. In countries such as America and Australia, however, the motor vehicle had substantially replaced the bicycle. There, the sudden enforced reliance upon pedal power for personal travel was a radical shift for many. Ultimately, people everywhere faced the same fundamental issues with respect to bicycles as they did with virtually everything else: where to get them—if they could be had at all—and how to keep them working.

As in other countries, the Australian government established wartime controls on motor vehicles, petrol, and spare parts and the population had to adjust accordingly. It was a jolt for Australians were heavily dependent

An NRMA road service patrol, Sydney, during World War II

Wheeling Matilda

upon the motor vehicle. By 1930 the nation ranked only behind the United States and New Zealand in per capita car ownership. Petrol rationing began in October 1940 and within a year private car owners received only enough fuel to drive about fifteen miles (24 km) per week. Some converted their motor cars to use charcoal or gas burners and within two years there were over 12,000 of these in New South Wales alone. Others simply stopped using their cars. From 1939 to 1942 vehicle registrations dropped by 16 per cent as the low petrol allowance made them uneconomical to license and maintain. And as in England and America, some Australians resorted to hoarding or acquiring black market coupons to keep going.

The public transport system was severely strained and mandatory 'queuing' was introduced to prevent passengers from rushing uncontrolled toward arriving trams, buses and trains. The government eventually reserved the buses for special classes of travellers, such as workers, and that put even more pressure upon the tram and train services. Film matinees finished by 4.30 pm so that moviegoers could leave the city before the workers. Taxi drivers, limited to 22 gallons (88 litres) a week, rarely took passengers anywhere from which they were unlikely to get a return fare. Thus late evenings in Sydney often meant a walk home across the Harbour Bridge for north side residents.

The basic transport mode for many was aptly summarised by an Adelaide headline: 'Bicycles Have a New Importance and Popularity in War-Time'. In Sydney the National Roads and Motorists' Association undertook its own war conservation effort by putting two road service patrols on bicycles to save petrol. The mechanics, with large tool boxes fitted above a small front wheel, pedalled about the inner city area helping motorists.

Within three months of the bombing of Pearl Harbor a detailed report on the Australian bicycle industry was produced. Children's models were immediately banned and all motorised bicycles were channelled to the armed forces. Wartime cycle production essentially centred about Bruce Small's Malvern Star operations. Small had travelled about Europe prior to

Above: Wartime conservation effort

Opposite: A Melbourne street during wartime rush hour

Malvern Star cycles bound for Allied Pacific forces

the war, studied the military bicycles of the Germans, French and Italians, and attempted unsuccessfully to sell the Australian military forces on the idea of adopting them. He advocated specially trained cycle corps which would not be susceptible to the impending petrol shortages.

When General Douglas MacArthur took command of the Allied Pacific Forces in Melbourne in 1942 he immediately ordered an increase in bicycle production, much to Small's surprise—the Yanks were among the last he thought would want them. The Malvern Star cycle factories, the largest in the southern hemisphere, were stretched to the limit. With overseas supplies cut off they had to begin producing some components for the first time in Australia. The tubular manufacturing facilities received military orders for radio masts, ambulance stretcher carriages, tent frames and radio location sets (which needed complex tubular structures). Staff increased from 400 to 726 and Small and his executives donned overalls to work three night shifts a week in addition to their managerial functions. Military cycle production in Australia reached its peak in 1943, along with a soaring domestic demand.

The Story of Australian Cycling

Malvern Star factory facilities

By the end of the war Australians were bicycling on a scale never seen before or since on the nation's streets and Malvern Star was proud of having kept 'the home tyres turning'.

Vietnam

Vietnam was wracked by fighting from the time of the Japanese occupation in 1940 until 1975. During that period the safety bicycle saw its greatest ever, and longest running, role as a military logistics tool—three-quarters of a century after its development. When it was all over, in 1975, the Vietnamese had been fighting the Japanese, French, Americans, or one another almost continuously for 35 years, longer than all the major wars of the century combined. In the process, Japan lost its dream of a Greater East Asia Co-Prosperity Sphere, the French lost a major element of their empire, and Australia and America lost their first war. Throughout it all rolled the bicycle.

For many Australians the Vietnam war was confusing. Among other things, it was about the capabilities and limits of technology. As the first television war it used the most sophisticated reporting technology available. But some believe that the cameras ultimately revealed little of the underlying problems and nature of the war. They focused one-sidedly upon the spectacular: napalm attacks, bombing patterns seen from above, soldiers firing at unseen targets, and the close up results of burnt villages, fleeing

The seat was removed and a stick inserted into the vertical tubing for pushing. Another stick was extended from the handlebars for steering

civilians, dead livestock, and body bags loaded onto helicopters.

In contrast there was little nightly footage from the enemies' perspective of Vietnamese bicycle porters carrying heavy loads down steep slopes, or climbing out of holes immediately after heavy bombing attacks to continue pushing heavily laden bicycles along muddy roads. Even if the networks had the footage, such scenes would have been too mundane for prime time news, night after night. Yet, those simple, unspectacular actions, repeated innumerable times around the clock, coupled with the determination to drive foreigners out of their homeland, were where the war was ultimately won. The traditional Australian and American military orientation—combat with an identifiable enemy—was thrown into disarray by North Vietnamese General Giap's mixture of ideological, political and military elements, in which soldiers and civilians dressed alike. Giap had not just altered the rules of the game, as Americans and Australians understood them, but had substantially changed its nature.

During it all, some portrayed the bicycle as a symbol of the conflict: peasant level technology against sophisticated weaponry and 'war management' techniques. Others dismissed the comparison and wrote derisively of 'that wish fulfillment of parlour-pink intellectuals, the soldier peasant wheeling his bicycle to victory'. But whether the bicycle was more than a symbol, or less than the key to victory, it certainly provided one basic lesson for all who wished to observe, think, and learn: the device was still a component of the military scene. It had not been made obsolete but was only overshadowed by other technological developments. Because those other technologies cast such dark shadows, however, the bicycle was left nearly invisible.

Anyone who served in Vietnam could not help but be aware of the millions of cycles in daily use which could, and did, serve equally well for civilian and military use. A perspective on that use was offered by Wilfred

The Story of Australian Cycling

Burchett, an Australian journalist who covered the war from the communist side in late 1963 and early 1964 and was widely published in European newspapers. The first westerner to travel the Ho Chi Minh Trail, Burchett was trusted so implicitly by the communist Vietnamese regime that the Australian government deemed him to be aiding the enemy and revoked his passport.

This is a two-cycle ambulance unit, with bamboo hung between the front and rear cycles to carry injured men in hammock-like stretchers. Also a pair of seats on each machine allowed four more to be carried. A man walked alongside each cycle, pushing

Several heavily camouflaged cycle porters

Burchett highlighted the flexibility of guerrilla travel by covering over 500 miles (800 km) by bicycle in just a few months in addition to extensive walking and riding in sampans. The riding conditions could be difficult: 'A narrow, winding trail, never more than three or four yards straight, with roots and snags everywhere; tiny stumps where the undergrowth had been slashed close to—but not level with—the earth, jabbing at your pedals and ankles; overhead creepers waiting to strangle you while you are looking down to avoid a stump; trellises of bamboo banging at your head no matter how low you bent over the handle bars; a multitude of spikes reaching out to rip your shirt and flesh'.

On exposed roads, a bicycle 'was better than being in a jeep because with the silence of bike travel we always had plenty of warning of approaching planes and could pull into the undergrowth'. With several bicyclists in a party he was sometimes warned to follow the next bicycle 'very precisely' because the road had been mined by the guerrillas with spiked or explosive traps. Burchett's most difficult times were when he had to cross the innumerable swaying bridges often made from narrow trunks of bamboo, carrying his bicycle across on his shoulders. He never failed to be surprised when 'cycling along a tiny crack through dense jungle, the cook would suddenly lean over and, without slackening speed, extract a chicken for my lunch [from the underbrush], its legs tied together with a bit of jungle creeper'.

It became obvious to Burchett that the communists could cut many Saigon-held roads and take control of many provincial and district centres, but had not done so because the roads were the guerrillas' supply lines and the towns their distribution centres. To capture them would draw South Vietnamese Army attacks and paralyse their own supply system.

The bicycle's widespread use in the growing war led Harrison Salisbury to raise the matter in October 1967 at a United States Senate Foreign Relations Committee hearing. He testified that communist supplies were bicycled to South Vietnam in such large amounts that 'without bikes they'd have to get out of the war', a point he had made in an article on the front page of *The New York Times* ten months earlier: The machine was 'as essential to the North Vietnamese as the auto is in Los Angeles'. As he observed, 'If by some magic weapon all the bikes in North Vietnam could be immobilised, the war would be over in a twinkling'.

Vietnamese crossing a rudimentary bridge

But there was no magic weapon. Just bewilderment for many allied soldiers and politicians at why they could not come to grips with an enemy which, as one Australian colonel described them, was using 'bicycles as utilities and elephants as five-ton trucks'. It is no wonder that in the end, when the television-informed public was trying to decide what it was all about, 'only the commercials made sense'.

7　A Racing Powerhouse

As the cycling craze swept the world and Australia in the 1890s, cycle racing—spectacular, exciting, glamorous, and dangerous—attracted huge crowds and money and Australia was no exception. Manufacturers and cycle race promoters invested tremendous sums in appearance fees and prizes, publicising events, and advertising their machines. Newspapers abroad not only had cycling columns but some devoted entire sections to the bicycle and bicycle racing. It was big business and money, fame, gambling and corruption followed.

Initially bicycle races (both ordinary and safety) were often held in conjunction with other activities such as agricultural shows, and riders were assigned racing colours (following the practice in horse racing). 'Half the charm of cycle racing to the general public is the beauty of the scene when a dozen or more riders in divers colours sweep along together.' These were soon abandoned for progressively briefer costumes and ensuing complaints about the 'skin tight singlet, a pair of trunks displaying the leg to the hip, and so tight as to expose the whole form'.

As the racing increased in popularity cycle meets quickly became

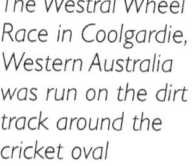

The Westral Wheel Race in Coolgardie, Western Australia was run on the dirt track around the cricket oval

exclusive events attracting immense crowds. In 1887 in Melbourne was initiated the Austral Wheel Race, now the oldest continuous track race in the world, and in 1895 the Melbourne to Warrnambool Classic, the second oldest road race. The legendary American rider, Arthur 'Zimmy' Zimmerman toured Australia in 1895 and in two appearances at the Sydney Cricket Ground drew nearly 60,000 spectators. About eight thousand persons, a significant proportion of the local population, turned out for Coolgardie's Westral Wheel Races on the Western Australian goldfields, for example, while in Melbourne in 1898 the ANA Wheel Races attracted a reported total of fifty thousand people, and in 1899 some sixty-five thousand. Sydney's and Adelaide's Cricket Grounds were likewise packed for major cycle races.

The crowds that turned up had a significant proportion of females, though they were not acceptable on the track. As *The Austral Wheel*, a staunch advocate of women's cycling, commented:

> That women's races will be held is unfortunately unavoidable, because there is a class of unmanly men which will derive pleasure from seeing girls with perspiring faces and heaving breasts 'riding all out' for some paltry prize or for a daily wage, as they lately did in London; and will look on with satisfaction while they are lifted half fainting from their machines, or are carried hurt and bleeding to the casualty room after a fall. And there are others who will get up such races for the sake of the gate money and the advertisement. We hope, however, that the best class of cyclists will discountenance the thing, and will let it be publicly known that they do so.

The most publicised cycliste activity was the visit of France's Mademoiselle Serpolette, 'the champion lady cyclist of the world', sponsored by the Gladiator cycling firm. As Australia had no one able (or willing) to match her she was essentially relegated to coaching at riding schools and giving demonstration rides. One writer said that she was certainly 'capable of shifting her machine to a lively tune … but with all due respects to Mademoiselle, we think the game unladylike'.

Some cycle firms and dealers, battling one another for any possible advantage in sales, subsidised riders and teams. As the philosophy was bluntly put, record setting and race winning meant sales, though the differences between most machines were negligible, if there was any at all.

While Dunlop had a near monopoly of tyre sales it still worked hard to preserve its position and was a major promoter.

Innumerable cycle tracks were found in locations ranging from major city centres to cleared areas in the bush, facilitated by the many large cricket and Australian football ovals which were adapted to racing at three laps to the mile. The track quality varied enormously. The Westral Wheel in Coolgardie was held on dirt and the Austral Wheel on grass at the Melbourne Cricket Ground. In contrast, surfaced cycle tracks were built around the Sydney Cricket Ground in 1896 and the Adelaide Oval in 1899, with the SCG adding lights for night racing in 1898. The financial benefits for the grounds' governing bodies were considerable. The Western Australian Cricket Association reportedly earned eighty per cent of its revenue for the period 1895-99 from cycle racing—almost as many persons were turning out for cycle training sessions at the ground in 1897 as turned out to see the inter-colonial cricket match.

The various track conditions and the furious riding resulted in intense racing and some spectacular and dangerous crashes. The hazards are summed up in an anonymous poem, 'To the 1897 Austral':

> After the Austral's over,
> After the track is clear —
> Straighten my nose and shoulders,
> Help them to find my ear.

The riding was hard and rough because there was much at stake, given the average annual income of the day (circa £120 in 1904). Victorian professional races alone distributed a reported £6,348 in total prize-money during the 1897-98 season and prize-money for single Australian races—£400 at the Westral and Austral Wheel Races, and £800 for the place-getters at the seven-race card of the ANA races of 1899, for example—ranked with that offered in North America or Europe. In addition, some firms paid separate awards; the winner of the 1898 Austral Wheel stood to pick up an extra £100 if he was mounted on a Swift bicycle. That was a lot of incentive to race and many riders tried their hand at it. In 1902 in New South Wales the League of Wheelmen issued 1,250 racing licences among its 71 clubs and 10,000 members. With so much money to be made, overseas riders visited the country as well.

Madamoiselle Serpolette

Cycle racing provided an alternative outlet for gambling and the money that changed hands resulted in prize-money paling into insignificance in comparison. Many seemed to accept the dictum that 'betting is the life and soul of any sport ... unless one had his "little bit" on the man of his choice one cannot raise three ha'porth of enthusiasm over such a race'. Technically

A pre-race lineup of riders at the 1896 Austral Wheel Race. It was run on grass at the Melbourne Cricket Ground

it was illegal to bet at most cycling venues, but the society, police and officials generally overlooked it. As to controlling gambling, one writer pointed out that 'The method adopted in Melbourne is to carefully notify by advertisement that care will be taken to suppress betting—otherwise some of the bookies might miss the fixture and go to the racecourse—and then to mark out special places for the ringmen to stand, by sticking up notices that betting is strictly prohibited'.

Unfortunately, even for those willing to accept gambling at cycle races, it became obvious that the racing was not a model of purity. The temptations, opportunities, and rewards accruing from race-rigging were too great to be ignored, and ultimately the cycling fraternity and the public never came to grips with the problem. Prophecies concerning its imminent demise were eventually fulfilled. The Austral Wheel Race of 1901, which involved large sums of money and dubious riding, resulted in widespread public criticism: 'It came to be realised that there was too much of unanimity of spirit amongst the riders; for the participants, at least, the placing had not the charm of the unexpected'. During the next couple of years the mass popularity of cycle racing declined markedly. The visits of Major Taylor in 1903 and 1904 would temporarily generate renewed interest, but it also highlighted the extent and nature of race-rigging and corruption.

Major Taylor in Australia

In 1904 the country witnessed one of the most amazing and controversial series of cycle races ever held when two avowed white racist Americans confronted the black American, Major Taylor, the world's best sprinter and highest paid athlete. Over a three month period, in connivance with Australian riders, they drove Taylor to a nervous breakdown and forced his retirement from cycle racing—at the peak of his career.

For one and a half decades, from 1896, spectators filled stadium after stadium in North America, Europe, the United Kingdom and Australasia to

Major Taylor (left) and Don Walker, the reigning Australian champion, Sydney, 1903

The Sydney Cricket Ground at night, 1903. The stands were lit by electric lights, and the track by overhanging gas lights. When the gun went off the electric lights were turned off, highlighting the lit track and riders

watch Major Taylor race. He was the highest paid and most famous athlete in the world's then most popular and lucrative sport. To give perspective, Honus Wagner's 1908 salary of $10,000 to play baseball in America is considered a landmark in American professional sports history. In 1903 Major Taylor had earned $50,000.

Marshall W. 'Major' Taylor, born in 1878, got his nickname from wearing a quasi-military uniform while performing riding stunts outside an Indianapolis bicycle shop to attract customers. Taylor proved to be far more than a stunt rider and his employer eventually entered him in a local race against white riders. He not only won but was soon setting sprint records.

The black teenager burst on to the world cycling scene in a spectacular manner by defeating Eddie 'Cannon' Bald, the reigning U.S. champion, in his professional debut at Madison Square Garden in 1896. There was no mistaking the message or the messenger. In 1898 Taylor won 21 of 45 races, came in second or third in the remainder, and won the World Sprint Championship in Montreal. U.S. sports writers proclaimed him America's cycling sprint champion. He was accorded the accolade again in 1899 and crowned official champion in 1900. The existence of rival cycling bodies led to disputed 'national champion' claims until that year. In 1901 Taylor went to Europe, beat the leading Continental riders, and was hailed as 'the fastest bicycle rider in the world'.

Taylor had two particular assets. One was a phenomenally strong and resilient character. He could not have accomplished what he did, in his day, without it. Second, because of his combination of ability and colour, wherever he went he consistently attracted larger crowds than any other cyclist in the world. If the Major made an appearance at a meet the promoter was essentially guaranteed financial success. Labelled 'The Ebony Streak', he was big business in his own right.

That ebony streak, however, created problems, for hovering over the Major was the intense racial prejudice in the United States. He was banned from riding at many tracks and subjected to racial slurs, on and off track. Finding a hotel that would take him in during his travels, or a restaurant near the velodromes that would serve him, was a constant problem, his fame notwithstanding. He was physically threatened by some of his white opponents and on the track many teamed up to prevent him from winning races. The bigotry, hatred and unfairness of his competitors eventually became intolerable, and ultimately forced Taylor off American cycle tracks and out of the country. Surprisingly, it was in Australia that it came to a head.

In 1902 a Sydney syndicate offered the Major £1,500 if he would race Down Under for just three months, creating The Sydney Thousand (£1000), the richest cycle race in the world, as incentive. He would also receive additional local appearance money and could keep all prize money that he won. The Major accepted and in November 1902 boarded the steamer SS Ventura, bound for Sydney. While on board he first heard of the 'White Australia Policy'. It was proudly proclaimed in the banner of *The Bulletin* as 'Australia for the Australians'; in 1908 it was altered to read 'Australia for the White Man', to allay any doubts. It caused Taylor great concern during the voyage but as he later summed it up, Australians welcomed him with a warmth, enthusiasm and spirit unlike anything he had ever known, and he received more pleasure from the tour than any other in his international racing career. On his first day of training at the Sydney Cricket Ground three thousand spectators applauded him as he pedalled onto the track.

The four month tour was also a marked financial success, as he walked

The Melbourne Exhibition Ground track, five laps to the mile, where Major Taylor suffered the worst fall of his career in 1904

away with the majority of prize money on offer that summer. Ominously, however, Major Taylor did not even qualify for the final of The Sydney Thousand, created specifically to attract and highlight his talent Down Under. The surrounding circumstances deeply disturbed many in the country, including Taylor himself. As The Sydney Sportsman wrote, 'there must be something in the sport of cycling that insensibly leads to crookedness'. There was. Money.

In Europe and North America most major cycle races were 'scratch' races. That is, everyone started from the same point. Handicap races tended to be reserved only for second rate riders and little prize money. In Australia, in contrast, handicap racing was more popular than anywhere else in the world, and was the format used for major races. The logic of handicap racing is simple. If one rider is markedly superior to all others, and all start from the same spot at the same time, the superior rider will finish first every time, other things being equal. In handicap racing, in contrast, the slower riders are given head starts, the amount depending upon their previous racing performances and general ability. Against Major Taylor, the slowest riders in some mile (1.6 km) races were given as much as a 200-yard (183 m) head start. If all went to plan, the racers would approach the finish line more or less at the same time, for an extremely exciting finish. In theory.

In reality, as with all bicycle racing, handicap racing suffered from the problem of wind resistance. Consequently, riders who were particularly close to one another when the gun sounded would quickly bunch up and alternately pace one another throughout the race. What resulted was that those near the back mark (the starting line) would tend to form a 'back bunch' and those further down the track, the 'front markers', would tend to form a 'front bunch'. The back markers paced one another in their attempt to close the gap with the front markers. Meanwhile, the front markers simply raced for the finish line as fast as possible and it became, in essence, a race between two groups. Whoever won the race would share a portion of his prize money with the others in his group, without whose help he could not have won. Australian riders had long accepted the concept.

The Major refused to make arrangements with anyone. As *The Advertiser* wrote, 'He always rides to win. He never sells a race'. When the gun went off Taylor quickly closed the short gap to the next riders who, being Australia's best, themselves started only slightly ahead of him. That fast back bunch soon caught the slower front bunch. With his ability Taylor would then sprint ahead of everyone near the finish to collect the first place prize money—and share none of it. Understandably many riders, without whose assistance he could not have won, did not appreciate it.

If Australia's top riders expected to win much money they had to figure out some way to stop the Major. One technique was to box him in such that he could not break free at the finish, but with his skill that was generally not effective. Ultimately it boiled down to preventing him from catching up with the front bunch by the other riders around him refusing to carry their share of the pacing burden. Neither of the tactics was team racing in the original Australian sense. They were outright attempts to defeat one man to others' benefit and that is exactly what happened at The Sydney Thousand semi-finals. The crowd increasingly booed the Australian riders in the back bunch as it became obvious they were not adequately pacing. The promoters and officials stopped the race half way through and ordered a re-ride. The result was the same and Taylor did not qualify for the final. As one journalist noted, 'Taylor was paid handsomely for coming to Australia, and they were under no obligation to assist him to win'.

Before Taylor arrived for a second Down Under tour in 1904 he was preceded by two intensely racist white Americans, Floyd MacFarland and his young protégé, Iver Lawson, who would win the World Championship six months later in London. MacFarland, at 6 feet 4 inches tall, was a striking figure with an immense range of talent. Known as the human motor 'He would win a sprint race one day, a pursuit and pace race the next, a six-day race and then ask the boys if they knew of any other games'. He not only won over 400 races in his career but, as a promoter and manager of several national and world champions, was one of the dominant influences on American and international cycle tracks for over two decades.

Floyd MacFarland was intelligent, shrewd, and well educated but directed substantial energy toward derailing the Major's career. Taylor said bluntly that MacFarland was 'the ringleader of the gang of riders who had sworn among themselves to bring about my dethronement'. Near the end of his life Taylor acknowledged that he had been taught that one should 'speak naught but good of the dead', but nonetheless he would always remember the late Floyd MacFarland as 'the instigator and leading perpetrator of practically all the underhanded scheming' that prevented him from winning another American championship. Sir Hubert Opperman described Floyd to me as 'an absolute bully, who was aggressive and bad-mouthed in every way. He was a first-class cyclist and a second-class citizen'.

The American duo, however, proved immensely popular with Australian cyclists, the promoters, and crowds. Australians appreciate and respect sporting talent and MacFarland and Lawson certainly had that in abundance. Everywhere they went people paid to see it. However, the pair quickly demonstrated a knack for leaving controversy in their wake. At the Westral Wheel Race in Western Australia, one of the three richest in the country, officials banned Lawson from the final for having 'pulled up' in a qualifying heat and allowing another rider to finish ahead of him. It was suspected that Lawson had deliberately thrown the race because he or MacFarland had bet heavily on the competitor. Iver's banishment from the final was no problem for the high-powered American pair, however. MacFarland simply mounted his machine and pedalled away with the £400 first prize.

But the most critical controversy Down Under swirled about the arrangements that MacFarland made to defeat Major Taylor. Given his force of character and ability to dominate other riders; his superb cycling

Iver Lawson (left, in suit) and Floyd MacFarland (centre cyclist) in Adelaide, 1904, with two other American riders

skills; his management of a highly gifted protégé; and his inclination to make arrangements, MacFarland found a fruitful field for exploitation. He emphasised that Major Taylor was already well paid for his Australian tour and would receive yet additional local appearance fees, aside from any prize money and bonuses. The other riders would ultimately end up doing the 'donkey work' only to watch the shrewd tactician and physically superior Taylor sprint around them at the finish, with no sharing of winnings. The implications were not lost on the Australians, and they now had to contend with MacFarland and Lawson as well. The local riders sensed the elemental truth in that old adage, 'if you can't lick them ...'. So they joined them.

It is not possible here to describe the 1904 season in detail, but Taylor, Lawson and MacFarland were a highly volatile combination and it got nasty, with pushing, shoving and elbowing routine. As one writer observed, 'Had [Taylor] not been a marvel of pluck, speed and skill, he would have either been killed outright or disabled ... Cycle racing is a very dangerous game, even under ordinary conditions, but when deliberate fouling is introduced, it is then too risky for even the most daring'. In one race, in frustration,

Taylor ran his pedal into MacFarland's front wheel, tearing out spokes and spilling him onto the SCG grass. In Melbourne Iver Lawson ran Taylor hard up against the wall on one of the sharp corners of a small, tight track. It was the worst fall of his career, with multiple lacerations.

In summary, Major Taylor effectively suffered a nervous breakdown at the end of the Australian tour, which he rated as the worst experience of his career, and withdrew from the sport at the peak of his form, international fame, and financial potential. The Major eventually recovered and rode from 1907-10 in Europe, but was never again a factor in American cycle racing. He eventually went broke through bad investments and died destitute in a Chicago charity ward in 1932. His body lay unclaimed for a week before finally being interred in the welfare section of a black graveyard.

Aussies Abroad

Before Major Taylor's visit few Australian cyclists went abroad and those who did were not particularly successful, though there was certainly no lack of quality Down Under. When Taylor toured Australia he ranked Don Walker, the reigning Australian champion at the time, among the ten best foreign riders he ever faced, but thought Australian riders were generally hindered in their development because of the prevalence of handicap racing in Australia.

Floyd MacFarland returned to Australia in 1905 and 1906, but by 1912 had turned his hand to full time race promotion and the management of tracks and riders, at which he was a master, and several Australians would be among the beneficiaries. He knew talent when he saw it and was instrumental in spotting and taking several of Australia's outstanding riders to America, where, as in Europe, the big money and international recognition lay. As Iver Lawson commented to an Australian scribe, Floyd 'knows exactly how to train a man, and he has taught me all I know. When I started with him I thought I knew a good deal, but soon found out that I knew nothing'. There was none better. Among the many riders MacFarland managed, Frank Kramer won 16 consecutive US national titles (1901-16) and Iver Lawson won the World Sprint Championship (1904).

Among the early big names benefitting from the MacFarland connection and support were Alf Grenda, 'The Tall Tasmanian', Alf Goullet

Australians, Alf Goullet (left) and Jackie Clark (centre) with Frank Kramer, who was U.S. national champion for sixteen consecutive years. Photograph circa 1916

from Victoria, and Reggie McNamara from New South Wales (spotted by Goullet and taken to America). Each individually won hundreds of races, and set various Australian, American and international records in anything from short sprints to the gruelling six-day races. All were major players on the international scene into the 1930s, particularly on the lucrative six-day circuits in the US and Europe. They were written up in major American magazines and earned tremendous amounts of money. Goullet, for example, earned $1,000 a day in the 1920s when, as Peter Nye, the American cycle racing historian, noted, a fledgling National Football League franchise could be bought for less. Several of the Australian riders eventually took up American citizenship and two of them, Reggie McNamara and Alf Goullet, were inducted into the U.S. Bicycling Hall of Fame. Their exploits are recounted in a video, 'The Six-Day Bicycle Races, America's Jazz-Age Sport', offering insights into a fascinating era and facet of cycle racing, in which the Australian riders were among key figures. 'Every six-day bicycle race', as one interviewee noted, 'was treated like a Superbowl today'.

Floyd MacFarland's death on 17 April 1915 (he was stabbed behind the ear with a screwdriver during a fight at a velodrome) marked the end of

Reggie McNamara was noted for hard riding and many falls. During his career he suffered concussions and broke his nose, leg, jaw (three times), collarbone (many times), and carried multiple scars.

an era. During the first 25 years of modern bicycle racing Floyd had been in the thick of it all and was the sport's premiere promoter when he died. MacFarland's funeral was attended by 1,500 people and *The New York Times* devoted two columns and a photograph to him.

It is beyond the scope of this book to chronicle Australian cycle racing and racers throughout the 20th century. It should be said however, that while the country was not a national force on the world's racing scene, several individual riders were among the best in the world in their day, such as Sid Paterson and Russell Mockridge at mid-century. Prior to that, Hubert

Opperman was one of Australia's most famous sports personalities in the 1920s and 1930s, and with the financial, administrative and personal support of Bruce Small, who owned Malvern Star bicycles, became one of the world's best long-distance cyclists. 'Oppy' won the prestigious Bol d'Or 24-hour race in 1928, the Paris-Brest-Paris road race in 1931, set a Land's End-to-John O'Groats record, and twice captained the Australian Tour de France team. In Australia he eventually owned nearly every long-distance cycling record and in 1939 he broke 101 state, Australian and world records during the course of a 24-hour non-stop cycling marathon at the old Sydney Velodrome, covering 489 miles (792 km) unpaced in 24 hours. Later he served as a Minister in the Menzies government and was knighted in 1968.

The Modern Powerhouse

Australia has managed to become a powerhouse on the present day world cycle racing scene through a combination of individual, local, state, national, organisational, and corporate support, along with rider commitment and determination.

There is more to the sporting world than the Olympics. However, it is the pinnacle of achievement for athletes in many sports, and national sporting pride is often measured by a country's Olympic success. Australia is no exception. In particular, the summer Olympics (the following discussion does not include the Winter Olympic Games) have a special significance Down Under because in the first modern Olympics in 1896 an Australian, Edwin Flack, won gold in both the 800 and 1,500 metre foot races. Australia is one of only two countries to have participated in all of the modern Olympics and has hosted the only two Olympics held in the southern hemisphere, in Melbourne in 1956 and Sydney in 2000. Overall, Australia is the tenth ranked nation in total Olympic medals won (467).

In the 1956 Olympics, Australians on their home ground won 35 total medals, third only to the Soviet Union and USA. The next couple of decades were golden for Australia's international sporting reputation, as runner John Landy became the second man to break one of track and field's landmark records, the four-minute mile; its swimmers generally maintained their world class performances (38 per cent of Australia's Olympic medals have been won in swimming and Australia and the USA between them have won

Wheeling Matilda

A participant in one of Australia's many present-day cycling events

45 per cent of all Olympic swimming medals). Australia's tennis players achieved legendary status, winning 35 of the 80 Grand Slam women's singles titles from 1960-79, while the men won 52 of the 80 Grand Slam men's singles in the 1950s and 1960s, and exactly half of the 120 played from 1950-79. In the cricket world Aussies have been a constant force and innovator in the game since participating in the first cricket Test Series in 1877, but as the sport is not played in much of the world, that success is not widely appreciated outside Commonwealth countries. For perspective, it should be noted that in 1980 Australia's population was 14,695,000, compared to the USA's 203,184,000.

In the early 1970s two reports were completed looking at the future of Australian sports, 'The role, scope and development of recreation in Australia' (1973), by John Bloomfield, and the 'Report of the Australian Sports Institute Study Group' (1975), chaired by Allan Coles. They were timely and influential, for in 1976 Australia came face-to-face with the realities of the modern sporting world. They won not a single Olympic gold medal in Montreal and a combined total of only five silver and bronze medals, a result considered by many to be a national embarrassment. As well, tennis players with names such as Navratilova, Nastase, and Kodes were the portent of the future. Since 1976 no Australian tennis player has won the Australian Open men's singles title and Australian men have won only five Grand Slam singles titles in total. No Australian woman has won the Australian Open women's singles title since 1979, and only two Grand Slam women's singles titles have been won elsewhere. Australians were facing the possibility of no longer being competitive in a world with an increasing number of international athletes and a proliferation of sophisticated sports science and training programs abroad. Various Australians began taking up offers to study in American universities to benefit from their training programs and the high level of competition to be found there (John Bloomfield himself obtained his PhD in 1968 at the University of Oregon).

The federal government established the Australian Institute of Sport, which opened on Australia Day, 1981. Its goal was to find, support and develop the best Australian athletes. The initial eight sports included were basketball, swimming, weightlifting, track and field, gymnastics, netball, soccer and tennis, selected because of their international prominence, potential for improvement and gender balance. A track cycling program was added in 1987, located at Adelaide.

Following pages: The Speed Dome, Western Australia

Wheeling Matilda

The Story of Australian Cycling

It was recognised that elite sport could not be separated from community sport, and successful junior programs were necessary for success at the elite level to be sustained. In 1985 an Australian Sports Commission was established, with the goal of working with national sporting organisations and community groups to improve sport in Australia at all levels. The original Commission and the AIS were amalgamated in 1988 (with formal legislation in 1989), with the AIS responsible for training facilities, sports science and coaching at the elite level. The Commission identified an overall strategic approach, plans and funding for national sporting organisations to provide effective development pathways for athletes.

Superb bicycling facilities were built around the country with enclosed indoor velodromes in Perth, Adelaide, Launceston, Melbourne, and two in Sydney. Brisbane cyclists continued using an outdoor cycling track at Chandler, but a new enclosed velodrome is being constructed on the Gold Coast for the 2016 Commonwealth Games. The facilities have been used to inspire both athletes and supporters, and for multiple uses. The Speed Dome in Western Australia (at Midvale, just east of Perth) is a good example of the community approach to development.

Australia, with its world powerhouse status, now attracts foreign riders Down Under for the high level of competition on offer. Track Cycling WA's Perth Winter Grand Prix, a world ranked event, includes riders from around Australia as well as Malaysia, South Africa, New Zealand, Taiwan, Singapore, and Hong Kong. Events include Sprint, Keirin, Scratch and Points races, as well as the feature event, the historic Westral Wheel Race, one of the world's oldest (since 1897). To encourage community involvement, the Winter Grand Prix integrates more than 1000 Cyclo Sportif riders into its activities, creating a 'Festival of Cycling'. The Cyclo Sportif is a series of rides created a decade ago which allow riders to participate in race-like conditions but without the competitiveness of formal road races. Several Cyclo Sportif rides are held annually in the Perth metropolitan area as well as regional locations. They are of varying lengths (e.g., 30, 60 and 90 kilometres) to cater to groups (of four to nine riders) ranging from novice recreational riders to those seriously interested in developing their team racing skills. However it is not a race, with no prizes awarded, and the entry fee includes a meal after the race.

The Cyclo Sportif start and finish is at the Speed Dome and the post-ride meal is a sit down affair on the back straight, as well as some 200

Post-Cyclo Sportif dining at the Speed Dome, Midvale, Western Australia

VIPs (corporate, patrons, etc.) hosted in the track centre. There is also a cycling trade show displaying goods, services, club contacts and food stalls. Through such major events, a couple of times a year, Track Cycling WA is able to generate both continuing and new support. As the Chairman Murray Hall noted, 'It works for us. We get a lot of new riders via that sales pitch'. Ongoing activities further generate and sustain that interest, with the venue used every day for junior cycling development, WA Institute of Sport training, school programs, ladies-only nights, adult entry level courses, corporate sessions and, of course, regular race nights. A skating rink is also incorporated into the middle of the track.

The AIS headquarters and a major training facility are in Canberra, the national capital, but various training venues are located elsewhere around the country. State-of-the-art facilities were built, top coaches, sports scientists, and administrators employed, and all-inclusive scholarships provided for the most promising athletes to enable them to train full time,

AIS European Traning Centre, Gavirate, Italy

including competition travel expenses, a crucial element given the country's distance from major competitions abroad which had long been an obstacle for Australian athletes.

Currently the AIS offers some 700 scholarships annually in 26 different sports. This includes an average of three dozen cycling scholarships, more or less equally allocated between men and women, in multiple riding categories. Athletes apply for scholarships, but the coaches in each sport have the discretion to offer immediate scholarships to any particularly promising up and comer. There are also scholarship programs for developing both coaches and officials as well as an effort to improve sporting participation at a broad national grass roots level. Online officiating and coaching courses assist both new and established coaches and officials around the country to improve coaching practices, and work with local sports programs and schools.

The combined national effort has paid off. Overall, 65 per cent of Australia's Olympic medals have been accumulated in the nine Olympics since Montreal, and in Sydney in 2000, Australia's 58 total medals tied it with China for third place, behind the USA and Russia, countries with immensely larger populations.

Australian cyclists have particularly benefitted from the combined effort of the Australian Institute of Sport, and Cycling Australia—the national governing body for bicycle racing Down Under and a member of the Union Cycliste International (UCI). Aside from Cycling Australia's headquarters in Sydney, the AIS track cycling program is located at the Adelaide Super-Drome, and in 1997 a cycling base was established in Tuscany in Italy, particularly for road cyclists, who spend much of their time in Europe. That was eventually integrated into an overall AIS European Training Centre at Gavirate, near Milan, catering not only to cyclists, but offering other Australian athletes reasonable access to a variety of European competition. Cycling Australia's efforts have also been supported by private companies and the public SBS television network's Cycling Central, which has various cycling programs and carries events such as the Tour de France live, as well as streaming many races from abroad.

The results have been little short of phenomenal. When the program was initiated Australia was rarely in the top two dozen ranked track cycling nations—by 1993 they were ranked number one. But success was also evident in every racing category. Between January and March, 2010, for example, Australia as a nation sat atop the UCI world rankings: Australian women held number one ranking in three of the eight Women's Elite track racing categories; Australian men topped three of the four Mountain Bike categories; and in BMX an Australian was the overall top ranked male rider, while Australians held three of the top eight women's positions. Australia's international cycling status was also recognised through South Australia's Tour Down Under being made the opening event on the annual UCI World Ranking calendar.

Over the last six Olympics (1992-2012) Australian riders have pedalled away with 34 medals, second only to Great Britain's 37, and more than any of the traditional cycling countries such as Germany or France, and more than Italy and the Netherlands combined. In the Tour de France, Aussie riders have finished second a half dozen times since 1998, five have worn the yellow jersey at some stage, and Australia's Cadel Evans won the Tour in 2011.

With support from Cycling Australia and the AIS, various riders have also been able to switch between categories to take better advantage of their talents. Stuart O'Grady, for example, has won track racing medals in two

> **PINCUS' Coca Jubes FOR.... CYCLISTS.**
> Invaluable for Long-Distance Touring and Racing.
> COCA is a Nervine & Muscular Tonic, relieving Hunger, Thirst, & Fatigue
> **S. PINCUS, Chemist, 5 Brunswick St., Fitzroy,**
> AND ALL CYCLE DEPOTS.

The Austral Wheel, December 1896

Olympics while being one of the great road riders of his era, and Cadel Evans won the UCI Mountain Bike World Cup cross-country championships in 1998 and 1999 before making the switch to road racing. Robbie McEwen was an Australian junior BMX champion before taking up road racing and eventually winning the Tour de France's green jersey (sprinter's classification) three times. Cycling Australia's role is no better epitomised than by its support for Anna Meares, who recovered from a broken neck in January 2008 to qualify for and win a silver medal in the Beijing Olympics six months later, and continue on to win various World Championships and Commonwealth and Olympic Games gold medals since.

Jim Ferguson, Executive Director of the Australian Sports Commission during the decade leading up to the 2000 Olympics, emphasised that it was the combination of an overall planned, systematic, national approach at both the elite and grass roots levels, together with the ground breaking scientific work of the AIS and its increased standard of coaching and athlete preparation, that turned Australian sport around. It required, as his book title suggests, 'More than Sunshine & Vegemite'.

Drugs

In researching the book Major Taylor in Australia, the issue of drugs never came up in any newspapers, cycle journals or sports magazines of that era, nor were there any doping agencies. On the other hand, as many advertisements of that era suggest, there were some commonly available and widely advertised and used stimulants. They ranged from some downright dangerous ones to various everyday drinks such as Coca-Cola, with its sugar, caffeine from the kola nut and, until 1904, cocaine from the coca leaf.

After conducting interviews for his book, *Hearts of Lions*, and those involved with six-day races well into the 20th century, Peter Nye summarised the situation simply: 'stimulants were just a part of doing business'. They ranged from relatively ineffective cognac and milk mixtures and ether on sugar cubes, to more potent concoctions involving cocaine and strychnine ('a central nervous system stimulant up to a certain point, and then it's lethal'), and eventually amphetamines. And pretty much everyone was using them, openly.

These stimulants, however, were to get a rider through a tough time, or to make it to the finish line on long races. The drugs of Major Taylor's era were not those of the performance enhancing dimension we have seen in recent times, such as anabolic steroids, EPO and HGH, which enable athletes to train harder and recover faster, to thus train even harder, more often and further build up strength and stamina. While stimulants enable one to push the body towards its limits, modern drugs allow athletes to extend those limits, but can involve some potentially unknown serious, long-term, and devastating side-effects, as the experiences of now middle-aged former East German athletes have shown.

With national prestige at stake and money and fame on offer for riders, manufacturers and sponsors, the temptation is always there to use drugs and many riders have been shown to have succumbed. How many more, and how often, has long been debated. But not in the mind of the French High Court judge who chaired the inquiry into the Festina racing team doping scandal in 2000; he told the French Senate inquiry in May 2013 that 'up to at least the end of the Armstrong era [2009] … one cannot believe for one instance in the fairness of the [Tour de France] races'.

The Lance Armstrong betrayal cost Americans the bragging rights of having the best ever in the business, and many cycle aficionados the loss of an idol. Australia is no exception. Within a recent nine month period three noted riders were exposed or admitted to doping at some time in their career. Between them they have won various World Championships, Olympic and Commonwealth games medals, ridden in 23 Tours de France (finishing second on four occasions), one has received a Medal of the Order of Australia (OAM) and another has been a national cycling coach and Sports Director of Australia's Orica-GreenEDGE professional cycling team. Such revelations of doping by riders at the pinnacle of the sport cast a continual pall over racing and intermittently renew the discussion of 'is it just an occasional bad apple?' or is the barrel itself rotten.

The Australian Legend

In 1897 W.B. Kimberley, in his *History of West Australia*, devoted one long paragraph to the use of the bicycle on the colony's goldfields, focussing upon the cycle express messenger riders. In the two-volume 1913 *Cyclopedia of Western Australia*, J.S. Battye devoted only five lines to cycling, which he inadequately described as having had a 'great vogue as a pastime'; in his 1924 history of the state he does not mention the machine at all. Frank Crowley's history, *Australia's Western Third* (1960), gave one sentence to the bicycle, referring only to its use by express riders. Until the publication of *The Bicycle and the Bush* in 1980, those four brief mentions represented the entire output on the use of the bicycle by professional historians in a state in which the machine was more important, and was adopted for more varied uses, over a longer period, than anywhere else in Australia and, in some respects, anywhere else in the world.

The most useful non-fiction writing on the bicycle in rural areas had been by those pioneering riders who documented their personal pedallings in the outback, such as Francis Birtles, Fred Blakeley, Bert James, Albert MacDonald, Jerome Murif, Frank Clune and Arthur Richardson. However, without an overview of Australian cycling history, the context and much of the significance of the rides was lost on later readers.

I have no definite answers to the question of why historians, writers and poets long ignored the bicycle's rural role (or urban, for that matter). However, I do offer the following observations. For one thing, the bicycle's physical presence was not imposing, the machine not always obvious in the landscape. Once the novelty of cycling wore off, the machine became just another commonplace item. Like the woodpile, pocket knife and billy-can, it was necessary, nearly ubiquitous, but of no particular concern. This view was reflected in the reaction of many of whom I requested interviews. They could not understand how they could be of help; all they had done was 'just ride an old pushbike'. Nor was it obvious on the printed page. John Merritt, who taught West Australian history at the University of Western Australia, once commented to me that he had been through those same WA history books and personal accounts of early life on the goldfields, and had researched in the very journals and newspapers from which I had drawn so many photos and relevant articles, but had never 'noticed' the bicycle. Thus by the time historians developed an interest in social history—'sober' historians had more important things to study, as J.S. Battye put it in 1913—the fact that the bicycle had been used significantly in rural areas was no longer common knowledge.

Much reportage of bush life in the heyday of bush cycling was by the influential school of writers associated with *The Bulletin*, the self-proclaimed, 'national Australian newspaper'. Their reaction to the introduction of safety bicycles was one of unremitting satire and disparagement. In fact, *The Bulletin*'s satirisation of the bicycle in Australian society provides some of the most pointed insights into the machine's impact.

'Banjo' Paterson, the prolific bush bard, is a case in point. The only known reference to bush cycling by Paterson is his famous poem 'Mulga Bill's Bicycle', a satirical look at a bushman's frustrated efforts to learn to ride the machine, published in *The Sydney Mail* on 25 July 1896. Paterson's biographer, Clement Semmler, told me that in researching his various books on Paterson he did not run across any other written reference by Paterson to bicycles. Yet, Paterson photographed an Australian Workers' Union Bicycle Corps at Coonamble in 1902 (pp. 92-93). The picture, showing at least twenty-two shearers on their machines, accompanied a long article Paterson wrote for *The Sydney Mail*. But, intriguingly, there was no comment on the Bicycle Corps in either the text or the accompanying caption. I suspect that Paterson, like so many others who visited the bush and wrote about the land and the people and their way of life, had a preconceived vision of what was there—and it did not include the bicycle. And he was not the only one. During the meeting with Clement Semmler (before *The Bicycle and the Bush* with its photo collection had been published), in which I sought his thoughts on why Paterson did not comment more on the bicycle's use in the bush, Semmler immediately, and with some degree of passion, pounded his clenched right fist into his left palm, saying, 'But it was not part of the bush. It was an inanimate object.' End of discussion, literally.

The shearer pedalling silently into town is unquestionably poor poetic fare. But Paterson's sole mention of bush cycling—and a poetic spoof at that—reminds me of nothing so much as James A. Michener's observation that Charles Russell, the American western artist, produced over 3,500 works and never once depicted a sheep.

The fact that the bicycle was widely used, particularly among unionised

The Bulletin, July 1897

shearers and itinerant workers, and was faster than the horse over long distances, was galling to many horsemen and squatters. The machine would not be ignored; it demanded a response. As bush cyclist Fred Blakeley observed, after the Mount Poole Station manager in western New South Wales once gave him very clear—but deliberately erroneous—directions: 'he hated bikes like hell. Strange as it may seem, all horsemen have this feeling towards push-bike men'.

In contrast to Paterson's view is the work of C.E.W. Bean (the WW I historian who was instrumental in the founding of the Australian War

Memorial) who travelled in western New South Wales in 1909 and wrote a series of articles for the *Sydney Morning Herald*, later published as *On the Wool Track* (1910). Bean refers to the use of the bicycle on several occasions and devotes a number of pages to the bicycle's use by shearers. Bean had returned to Australia only five years before, after having lived for fifteen years in England. By his own admission, he had never met a rouseabout, shearer, drover or boundary rider, and he would not read (or recall having heard of) Tom Collins' *Such is Life* for another thirty-five years. Ken Inglis, in his brief biographical sketch, suggests that Bean was 'uncertain about his own identity' and spent the period from 1904 to 1914 making 'his own discovery of Australia'. As is the case with so many visitors and returning expatriates, they often perceive acutely what the resident takes for granted. The heavily laden bicycles, the country in which their riders travelled, and the great distances, all fascinated the long-term English resident. Bean's book conveys a great sense of wonder at the nonchalant accomplishments of bush cyclists: 'The shearer set out on these trips exactly as if he were going from Sydney to Parramatta. He asked the way, lit his pipe, put his leg over his bicycle, and shoved off.'

In a country steeped in a Centaurian tradition centred about the stockman and drover, the appearance of the bicycle—however utilitarian or ubiquitous—struck an incongruous note with many. Thus the flavour of the bush bikers' relatively brief heyday has been substantially lost through the failure of contemporary historians, writers and poets to portray its use. That is unfortunate. But to recognise the fact that bush cyclists were ignored has implications about the accuracy with which other, perhaps more subtle, aspects of the bush were reported and manipulated during the shaping of the Australian Legend.

One last comment. In 1973 the poem 'Mulga Bill's Bicycle' was featured in a lovely book illustrated by Kilmeny and Deborah Niland. They won an award for their artistry, and deservedly so. However, they put Mulga Bill on a penny-farthing, thus missing the point of Paterson's poem. I wrote to the publisher (then Collins, now HarperCollins) pointing out the error and they responded with a spoof of Paterson's spoof, beginning something to the effect 'Twas a learned young man from Canberra…' (sadly, I have lost it over the years). They did, however, still offer to publish my book. Unfortunately, even though Wikipedia acknowledges that Mulga Bill would have been riding a safety machine, several subsequent illustrated versions of Mulga Bill have also shown him on a penny-farthing. One was even published as part of a literacy series by Oxford University Press, publisher of *The Bicycle and the Bush* book, in which the error was originally noted. The following sketch will provide a guide for future illustrators.

'Twas Mulga Bill, from Eaglehawk, that caught the cycling craze;
He turned away the good old horse that served him many days;
He dressed himself in cycling clothes, resplendent to be seen;
He hurried off to town and bought a shining new machine;
And as he wheeled it through the door, with air of lordly pride,
The grinning shop assistant said, 'Excuse me, can you ride?'

'See, here, young man,' said Mulga Bill, 'from Walgett to the sea,
'From Conroy's Gap to Castlereagh, there's none can ride like me.
'I'm good all round at everything, as everybody knows,
'Although I'm not the one to talk—I hate a man that blows.
'But riding is my special gift, my chiefest, sole delight;
'Just ask a wild duck can it swim, a wild cat can it fight.
'There's nothing clothed in hair or hide, or built of flesh or steel,
'There's nothing walks or jumps, or runs, on axle, hoof, or wheel,
'But what I'll sit, while hide will hold and girths and straps are tight;
'I'll ride this here two-wheeled concern right straight away at sight.'
'Twas Mulga Bill, from Eaglehawk, that sought his own abode,
That perched above the Dead Man's Creek, beside the mountain road.
He turned the cycle down the hill and mounted for the fray,
But ere he'd gone a dozen yards it bolted clean away.
It left the track, and through the trees, just like a silver streak.
It whistled down the awful slope, towards the Dead Man's Creek.

It shaved a stump by half an inch, it dodged a big white-box:
The very wallaroos in fright went scrambling up the rocks,
The wombats hiding in their caves dug deeper underground,
But Mulga Bill, as white as chalk, sat tight to every bound.
It struck a stone and gave a spring that cleared a fallen tree,
It raced beside a precipice as close as close could be;
And then, as Mulga Bill let out one last despairing shriek,
It made a leap of twenty feet into the Dead Man's Creek.

'Twas Mulga Bill, from Eaglehawk, that slowly swam ashore:
He said, 'I've had some narrer shaves and lively rides before;
'I've rode a wild bull round a yard to win a five-pound bet,
'But this was sure the most awful ride that I've encountered yet.
'I'll give that two-wheeled outlaw best; it's shaken all my nerve
'To feel it whistle through the air and plunge and buck and swerve.
'It's safe at rest in Dead Man's Creek, we'll leave it lying still;
'A horse's back is good enough henceforth for Mulga Bill.'

> A.B. Paterson, 'Mulga Bill's Bicycle',
> as printed in *Rio Grande's Last Race*,
> Angus & Robertson, 1902

9 The Bicycle Today

In 1897 bikes were mostly the same basic diamond frame design (along with women's step through models). Today's bike shop would boggle a bushie with the range of models and terminology—BMX, cargo, cruisers, cyclocross, folding, hybrid, recumbent, road, track, and triathlon. So would the prices of some of the exotic models incorporating highly sophisticated technology and materials. A trade representative commented that some categories, such as mountain bikes, are now so highly specialised—downhill mountain bikes, cross-country mountain bikes, and urban mountain bikes (yes, you read that right)—that it is hard to qualify them as a group any longer. Even fixed wheel bicycles are back in vogue as 'fixies'. In terms of performance some machines are hardly recognisable to someone who hasn't ridden in a couple of decades, with disc brakes, shock absorption systems, sophisticated gearing, electronic shifting and weighing very little.

Wertheim Cycle Depot, Collins Street, Melbourne, 1898

The Story of Australian Cycling

99Bikes, Chermside, Queensland, 2013

A notable recent development in cycle technology is the electric assisted bicycle, or ebike. Electric bicycle patents were registered in the 1890s but it was only with the advent of modern high capacity batteries and the development of controls and torque sensors in the 1990s that they became practical. Their adoption was explosive in China, with some 120,000,000 in use within one and a half decades, and they now represent a significant and rapidly increasing percentage of bikes in many cities around the world. With ebike users' average cycle trips being nearly double those of non-electric cyclists, there are considerable implications for future travel patterns.

Ebikes have particular advantages for users such as Australia Post. Bicycles were employed by the mid-1890s for telegram delivery and in Melbourne from July 1898 for collecting mail from pillar boxes throughout the city. Fourteen bicycles and eighteen men worked in shifts to clear the boxes, with one cyclist doing what formerly required a team of horses, wagon, teamster and box clearer. The Postmaster-General introduced bicycles throughout Australia on a large scale at the end of the First World War. In 2011 it purchased 1,000 electric bicycles. They cost less than motor bikes and maintenance and running costs are lower. A single charge

Telegram delivery, Cootamundra, New South Wales, 1896

can comfortably handle a heavy load and rider on an average daily delivery route of three to five hours, and the batteries last well over a year before requiring replacement. Two important factors are that it has been difficult to recruit adequate numbers of staff with motor bike licences (not required for electric bikes), and ebikes do not require registration. Australia Post anticipates using more in the future.

'Surprisingly little, though, has changed with bicycles', as one cyclist put it. 'It is still two wheels and a crank, with a saddle and handlebars'. What has changed is the role of the bicycle in Australian society. After World War II its use for commuting to work and general daily travel declined markedly. Towns and cities began sprawling out, made possible by and requiring increased motorised travel. The bicycle became a less viable, safe, attractive and socially acceptable transport form. Such legendary Australian cycle manufacturers as Malvern Star and Speedwell succumbed to a downturn in post-WW II sales, economic readjustments and a rationalisation of the industry; they were bought out in 1958 and 1965, respectively (Malvern Stars are still sold, but the company is now foreign owned). By 1970 Australian cycling had probably reached its nadir. Australian manufacturing was replaced by foreign imports, and cycling substantially relegated to children, many of whom still rode bikes to school in significant numbers, and for sport and recreational use.

During the latter 20th century there was a resurgence in cycling interest. Added to the continuing market for children's bicycles (they account for about a third of annual sales) was an expanded realm of recreational riding such as BMX, off road and mountain biking. As well, more sophisticated machines, increasing environmental concerns and the growth of cycling organisations led to a renewed popularity and use of bicycles. It has shown no signs of abating and from 2002 through 2013 some 15,000,000 machines were bought, more than the number of motor cars sold during that period.

Electric Vehicles Pty Ltd custom-designed AusPost electric bicycle, 2013

The Better Life

Australia is relatively wealthy, with the OECD ranking it fifth in the world in terms of average wages. That wealth has enabled Australians to own motor cars—lots of them. As previously noted, Australia was among the earliest and most enthusiastic adopters of the motor vehicle. By 1930 its per capita ownership was exceeded only by the United States and New Zealand and the three countries have not let anyone catch up. Ignoring minuscule, crammed entities like San Marino, Monaco and Liechtenstein, among others, the United States, New Zealand and Australia still are the highest per capita owners of motor vehicles in the world, according to the World Bank.

Australia's car centricity is understandable, given the country's vast area and large distances. However, its population is among the most urbanised and highly concentrated in the world. Excluding island and city states such as Hong Kong, Singapore and Nauru, Australia's 89 per cent urbanisation rate is exceeded only by Uruguay, Argentina and Japan. The three sprawling metropolitan areas of Sydney, Melbourne and Brisbane-Gold Coast collectively accommodate half the nation's population. Anyone who has travelled in any of them during rush hour needs no international organisation to tell them that these cities hold their own when it comes to traffic congestion.

But there is more to life than economics. According to the OECD's Better Life Initiative (a detailed survey of 24 indicators in 11 categories, including economic factors), Australia has ranked first among all developed countries for two years in a row, and variations on such surveys over the years routinely put the country at or near the top. That's the good news. Among the bad news is the fact that Sydney's weekend traffic on many roads is now as bad as, or worse than, weekday rush hours as its residents partake of that better life

And partake they do. The Australian Bureau of Statistics recently released data from the most comprehensive study of Australians' health yet undertaken: 63 per cent are now overweight or obese. While America tops the list of obese nations in the developed world—at 31 per cent, and that is obese, not just overweight—Australia managed sixth, with 25 per cent, according to the World Health Organisation. As well, one

George Street, Sydney, then ...

in four children between two and sixteen years of age are overweight or obese. Over half of Australians either do not exercise at all, or not enough for it to have any significant health effect. It is not surprising to find high incidences of heart disease, diabetes, high blood pressure and high cholesterol.

A 2011 National Cycling Participation Survey found that seventy per cent of Australians eighteen years or older had not climbed on a bicycle at all during the previous year, nor 83 per cent in the past month. Furthermore another study found that 'the Australian population aged nine years and over grew by 58% between 1986 and 2006 and the daily average number of bicycle trips grew by only 21%, representing a net decline in cycling'. While the absolute number of riders has increased, it suggested that a million more people would be riding if Australians now cycled at the same rate as in the mid-1980s.

Many of those 15,000,000 bicycles (plus who knows how many still operable pre-2002 machines) seem to be collecting dust in the garage.

... and now

From Marginal to Mainstream

Australian cycling is going through a transition from being a marginalised minority activity—primarily for sport and recreation—to a mainstream transport option. The bicycle is still considered by many to be a lifestyle accessory, but its general use is on the rise. Increasing numbers of jobs and high density residences in and around the central cities mean more people live within ready cycling distance of their work. The establishment of long cycle ways enable commuters to pedal from further afield. And many taking up recreational riding discover (or rediscover) its day-to-day travel potential.

The transition is difficult for the decision-makers, planners and traffic engineers who have to allocate funds and make plans for limited, crowded road space. Large numbers of motorists, bus users and pedestrians neither cycle nor give any consideration to the potential of cycling transport. To them the investment of money and diversion of space and facilities to cyclists, whom they see as a minority, can seem inequitable. And as political power, sentiments and philosophies shift from time to time, so does enthusiasm for, and investment in, cycling facilities and planning. There is controversy and tension between those who can see the vision and possibilities and those who can't.

In the struggle for contested urban space and the need to move as many people as cheaply and efficiently as possible, the bicycle has come a long way in the last few years as an accepted part of the planning process. London's mayor recently announced a billion pound commitment over ten years to advance cycling in that city, an effort applauded and acknowledged in international cycling and urban planning circles. Relatively unheralded Brisbane is in the midst of an eight year program that is spending more per capita than will London.

The major barrier to the use of the bicycle as an urban transport tool in Australia today is the perceived and actual dangers of riding in traffic. That fact comes up in study after study. Where increased cycling infrastructure makes riding easier and safer, there has come increased ridership. The City of Sydney recently saw over a doubling in the number of cycling trips in 36 months following completion of substantial facilities. Such results clearly indicate a latent demand—leaving many Australians frustrated that additional funds haven't been committed to exploiting that demand more quickly.

Cyclists account for seventeen per cent of morning peak traffic along Albert Street, East Melbourne

Those who understand the implications for the current state of the nation's health realise the need to promote healthier travel in Australia. The federal government's recent release of a ministerial statement on active travel reflects that. Increased emphasis is proposed for both public transport (which encourages walking to and from the local bus stop or railway station) and the use of bicycles. It won't be easy, for children today have a very different experience, sense and expectation of getting around than did many of their parents. Some sixty per cent are now driven to and from school, in contrast to about ten to twelve per cent in 1970. Unfortunately, for whatever reason—perceived stranger danger, parental convenience, that walking and cycling are unsafe or too slow—many of those children who walked and cycled three decades ago are the very ones now chauffeuring their own offspring.

Some efforts at promoting cycling have not been successful. Two ambitious bike share schemes in Australia were launched in 2010 in Brisbane and Melbourne. After three years they have attracted far fewer riders than

ArtBikes, Hobart

anticipated. Several observers feel that the intent is fine but the country is probably not yet ready for them. It needs a changed community mindset towards using bikes for short transport trips, and better infrastructure to make such use safer in city traffic. Two other limited bike share schemes are in operation in Australia. The country's first, launched in Adelaide in 2005, is not a basic element of the local transport scene, but used mostly by tourists. Hobart also instituted a tourist-focussed ArtBike scheme in 2011 to enable visitors to get around the city and waterfront area's museums and not-for-profit galleries.

Advocacy

Cycling is in a much better position than it was thirty years ago partly because of good advocacy. A major step was the establishment in 1979 of the national Bicycle Federation of Australia (it lasted until 2010). Through active recruitment of members (Bicycle New South Wales enrolled nearly 10,000 members in the 1980s, for example) both the Federation and state groups gained clout. In 1998 Bicycle Victoria, now known as Bicycle

Network, withdrew and independently developed the largest Australian bicycle organisation (and one of the largest such in the world), approaching 50,000 members nationwide. It supports and provides services to several other state cycling organisations and its *Ride On* magazine is now the de facto national periodical. Its instigation of various activities and push for improved facilities has been of great benefit to cycling as a whole.

Bicycle Industries Australia, the association for wholesalers, manufacturers and distributors, established the Cycling Promotion Fund in 2000. It is an independent organisation to promote the health, environment, transport and social benefits of cycling. Attention was focussed at the federal level in 2009 with the establishment of the first formal national cycling advocacy position, with a registered lobbyist. The goal is to develop non-partisan relationships with all sides of politics, and provide objective research, data and positioning with respect to cycling matters. A website was recently created for federal political candidates to post their policy on cycling issues, with an objective of establishing a nationwide cycling constituency in the federal political arena.

The online world and its internet forums have become increasingly important in the exchange of ideas, information, and enabling individuals to find and coordinate with others. Many local bicycle user groups have evolved at a relatively grass roots level to support bicycling activities and advocacy. Cycling advocacy is not limited to cycling organisations. Many influential executives, professionals, planners, traffic engineers and politicians who now cycle bring their influence to bear, often behind the scenes. Government entities lobby and negotiate with one another in developing bike strategies, plans and cycle way routes. As well, groups like AustCycle and the Amy Gillett Foundation run national programs in an effort to eliminate bike-related fatalities, provide riding and safety skills, and encourage more bicycling.

Helmets

In 1972 Australia was the first country to mandate the wearing of seatbelts in motor cars by all passengers. It was so immediately and measurably successful in reducing deaths and injuries that many other countries quickly began following suit. Australia also led the way with mandatory bicycle

An essential section of every Australian bicycle shop

helmet legislation and by July 1992 all cyclists had to wear one. Other countries' national and local authorities have instituted bicycle helmet laws to varying degrees, particularly for children. Few, however, have made them mandatory for all riders, notably New Zealand in 1994 and Israel in 2007 (which in 2011 repealed part of the law). While Australia led the world with its helmet legislation, the world is not following.

The legislation resulted in a marked decrease in ridership among certain segments of the population and inhibits a number from taking up riding today. It has been the subject of much research, argument and debate in Australia and abroad. Many feel that it was an unfortunate move, a mistake that set cycling back, and has made it much more difficult to achieve mainstream cycling normalisation in Australia. It is also argued that mandatory helmet wearing unfortunately places cycling within the realm of such risky and dangerous activities as white water rafting, mountain climbing, abseiling and parachuting—and questions whether bike riding belongs there. Certainly helmets should be worn for such highly risky activities as mountain biking and road racing, but recreational cycling on a bike path or riding to the store? Most of the world cycles without helmets.

The mandatory law is strongly supported by those who believe that cycling is an inherently risky activity and helmet wearing should override other considerations. After twenty years of a mandatory law and an entire generation of children having grown up with it, there is a strong sense among many riders and non-riders alike that they must be worn as a matter of community and personal responsibility. There are other countries that have various helmet laws but perhaps none so zealously enforced by the populace that, as one rider noted, 'if you ride down a street in Melbourne without your helmet, people will occasionally lean out of their cars and yell, "where is your helmet?" at you'. The bottom line for many is that the law is so solidly ingrained and arguments simply so divisive and inconclusive that debating it is a waste of time and energy that could be more profitably spent on other matters.

The law is not universally enforced around the country, however, and a noted Australian health and medical professional reviewed numerous studies and concluded that 'the health benefits of cycling (through increased physical activity) significantly outweigh the injury risk.' As cities implement and improve cycling infrastructure and ridership increases, there will likely be pressure to re-examine the helmet law. Various city officials have signalled that they would seek an exemption at least for adults using future public bike share systems. There are those who also think there is merit in trialling other exemptions in a staged fashion, such as when riding on paths/shared paths, or on roads with low speed limits. In any case it will take a convinced, committed and brave public official to relax the legislation, to whatever degree.

Conclusion

Thus stands bicycling in Australia today, 100 years after Percy Armstrong completed the first transcontinental bicycle ride in Melbourne and cyclist messengers began pedalling about the Western Australian goldfields.

So what of the future? That can only be known by those who will be there, for predictions are notoriously difficult. In the latter 20th century a number of people prophesied that the 21st century would be the Japanese century, economically. It appears they missed the target by 700 kilometres

(420 miles). China at that time was only a small blip on the economic radar, with the bicycle a staple and symbol of the country. Today it is second only to America in economic power. As the residents climbed into automobiles and on motor bikes and motor scooters, bike lanes were closed in some cities and Shanghai banned cyclists from some streets as obstacles to the freer flow of motorised traffic. The number of bicycles in use nationally declined by a third in a recent decade, with the numbers ridden in Beijing dropping more than half.

For inspiration and lessons as to what the bicycle could become in Australian society some look abroad to such cities as Copenhagen, where a large percentage of households do not own a car and a substantial proportion pedal about their business. However, the Sydney metropolitan area is almost one third the size of the entire country of Denmark and any lesson will require adaptation to Australian conditions, to use a time honoured cliché.

But surprising things happen. In China, air pollution and congestion contributed to a sharp turnaround in government policy in just a handful of years, leading to the establishment of its vast bike share schemes (over half a million bikes in total) and the ongoing massive adoption of electric bikes. Copenhagen's high cycle ridership did not simply happen, either. It required a commitment to a formal bicycle strategy and the ongoing planning and implementation of a major infrastructure over decades. If bicycles are to make a dent in Australia's health status or urban congestion, similar steps are required. Whatever happens here, impetus will have to come from within and, as in other places, will take time, and will be akin to turning a super tanker around by pedalling the tugboat.

In Australia the bicycle will not go away. It is just not clear as to which way it will go.

Acknowledgements, sources and bibliography

I wish to thank those who made this book possible. My wife Roey was the editor, critic, book designer, and drew the illustration of Mulga Bill on page 164. My son Russell copy edited and my brother Gary inspired the perfect title.

Portions of the final chapter are based upon interviews with Australians who have devoted a part of their lives to the bicycle and its use. Among them are professional planners, transport strategists, advocates, cycling group members and officers, magazine founders and editors, cycle trade executives, and competitors. I thank them for their enthusiasm and trust that my synthesis has done justice to their range of observations and comments. They are Harry Barber, Graham Bradshaw, Fiona Campbell, Robyn Davies, Elaena Gardner, Christian Haag, Stephen Hodge, Margaret Howard, Neil Irvine, Omar Khalifa, Mary McParland, Robert Moore, Jeremy Murray, Daman Rao, Renee Smith, Russ Webber, and Ben Wilson.

Many helped in various ways by reading sections or providing information, photos, leads and valuable assistance. They include Michelle Adler, Stuart Baird, Jeremy Betts, Russell Chapman, Scott Dickason, Jill Farish, Jim Ferguson, Jeff Groman, Murray Hall, Alexandra Koutts, Dianne Nguyen, Peter Nye, Warren Salomon, Michelle Skehan, Iain Treloar and Simon Vincett.

For the last chapter a wide variety of sources were canvassed. A number of facts and information relating to current Australian cycling matters was provided by interviewees. Additional sources include 'Australian National Cycling Participation, 2011', Sinclair, Knight Merz, August 2011; Chris Gillham and Chris Rissel, 'Australian per capita cycling participation in 1985/86 and 2011', in *World Transport Policy and Practice*, May 2012, pp. 5-12; Sherley Wetherhold, 'The Bicycle as Symbol of China's Transformation', *The Atlantic*.com.au 30 Jun 2012; 'Australia: the Healthiest Country by 2020', A discussion paper prepared by the National Preventative Health Taskforce, 2008; and Chris Rissel, 'Wrong-headed laws', *MJA InSight*, 23 April, 2012. For agency sources cited in the text, such as the OECD, World Bank, and Australian Bureau of Statistics, updated information (depending upon when you are reading this book) can be had by wandering through their websites.

Many people and institutions over the years have been instrumental in helping me pull together the broad outlines and innumerable details of Australia's cycling history. Prior to the publication of *The Bicycle and the Bush* (Oxford University Press, Melbourne, 1980) little had been written on the topic. Although concerned principally with bush cycling, the original bush book is the most thorough study yet of the use of the bicycle in this country. It was adapted from my 1979 Australian National University PhD thesis, 'The Bicycle in Rural Australia: A study of Man, Machine and Milieu'. The few earlier works surveying the general cycling scene in Australia in the early days were F.G.C. Hanslowe's single issue of the *Australian Cycling Annual* (1897); Leonard Henslowe's *Cycling: The Sport and Pastime* (1897); and E. Lincoln's *New South Wales Motorists' and Cyclists' Annual 1905*. Later surveys of one or another aspect of Australian cycling history included Keith Dunstan's chapter, 'The Pedalling Passion', in his book *Sports* (1973); Gordon Inglis's brief chapter on cycle racing in his *Sport and Pastime in Australia* (1912); and. H. 'Curly' Grivell's *Australian Cycling in the Golden Days* (1951), a collection of biographical sketches of early racing cyclists. Hubert Opperman, one of the world's top racers of his day, and one of Australia's great sports heroes, presents an interesting and highly informative perspective upon the Australian and international cycle racing scene of the 1920s and 1930s in his book *Pedals, Politics and People* (1977). My chapter, 'The Spectrum of Australian Bicycle Racing: 1890-1900', in *Sport in History* (1979), describes the heyday of Australian cycle racing.

A number of accounts of individual cycle journeys were published. George Burston's and H.R. Stoke's *Round About the World on Bicycles* (1890) is good reading as both a cycling adventure and travelogue. Jerome J. Murif's *From Ocean to Ocean: Across a Continent on a Bicycle* (1897) and The Austral Cycle Agency's pamphlet, *Albert MacDonald of Ororoo* (1898), both discuss the Darwin-Adelaide rides. Arthur Richardson's *Story of a Remarkable Ride* (1900) describes the main events of his around-Australia ride of 1899-1900, and the journey of Alex and Frank White and Donald Mackay during the same period is discussed in considerable detail in Frank Clune's *Last of the Explorers: The Story of Donald Mackay* (1942). Fred Blakeley's 1908 ride from Milparinka, NSW., to Darwin is recounted in *Hard Liberty* (1938). Francis Birtle's books, *Lonely Lands* (1909) and *Battle Fronts of Outback* (1935) together provide an excellent perspective upon the use of the bicycle in isolated areas.

To learn about the early Australian cycling scene it is necessary to read the cycling journals. The first ones were sporadic in publication and spotty in coverage. These included, in the 1880s, *Bicycle*, *Bicycling News* and *Australian Cycling News*. In 1893 the *Australian Cyclist* began; it achieved national circulation and was the longest running of all the journals, lasting well into the 20th century. The other journal with some semblance of national circulation, and by far the best in the country (broad coverage and good writing and technical production), was the *Austral Wheel*, published in Melbourne from 1896-1900. It included articles on touring, social and technical matters, the early introduction of motor vehicles, national and international cycling news, and racing (although downplayed). Other journals tended to be localised in their coverage and distribution: the *South Australian Cyclist*; the *West Australian Wheelman* and *WA Cyclist*; *Cycling Times*; the *New South Wales Cycling Gazette*; *Wheelman*; and a reputed *Queensland Cyclist*, of which I could find no issue.

Cycling was given good coverage in general sporting periodicals. By the late 1890s many newspapers and magazines included a cycling column, usually in the sports pages, as well as general articles about cycling events and activities. The regular cycling columns proved a mine of information; I found the *Morning Herald* (Perth) particularly useful for my purposes. In some newspapers, 'The' is part of the title, and in others it is not. For consistency I have deleted the word in every case. Others in which I found valuable material were *Advertiser* and *Observer* of Adelaide; *Age*; *Argus*; *Australasian*; *Bell's Life in Western Australia*; *Broad Arrow Standard*; *Bulletin* (Sydney); *Bulong Bulletin*; *Miner, Pioneer* and *Review* of Coolgardie; *Daily Telegraph* (Sydney); *Dunlop Gazette*; *Eucla Recorder*; *Grafton Examiner*; *Kalgoorlie Miner*; *Kanowna Democrat*; *Leonora Miner*; *Menzies Miner*; *Miner's Right* (WA); *Melbourne Punch*; *Moruya Examiner*; *Mount Magnet Miner and Lennonville Leader*; *Murchison Miner*; *Newcastle Sun*; *Sydney Morning Herald*; *Smith's Weekly*; *Sydney Mail*; *West Australian Review*; *Western Argus*; *West Australian*; *Western Mail*; *Western Star* (Roma, Qld); and the *Worker* (Brisbane and Sydney versions); *Arrow* (Sydney); *Canterbury Times* (Christchurch); *Herald* (Melbourne); *Narandera Argus* (it is spelled correctly, for those Australians who know it as Narrandera today); *Narandera Ensign*; *Newcastle Herald*; *Sunday Times* (Sydney); *Sydney Sportsman*; *Star* (Sydney); *Town & Country Journal* (Sydney); *Truth* (Melbourne); *Wagga Advertiser*; *Wagga Wagga Express*; *Weekly Press* (New Zealand); and *Weekly Times*.

Several private diaries recording long cycle journeys were made available to me: Arthur Richardson's 1896 crossing of the Nullarbor; Bert James's 1897 ride from Mount Magnet, WA to Melbourne; J. 'Scotchy' Wright's 1898 Nullarbor crossing; the Rev. A. Sussex's various rides during the period 1900-03, while serving as minister on the Western Australian goldfields; J.W. Dodgson's 1904 ride from Murat Bay, SA, to Southern Hills Station, WA; and Felix Keatley's 1909 journey from Black Rock, SA, to southwest Queensland, along the Strzelecki Track, with his shearing mates.

Special mention must be made of the Dunlop records held by the Archives of Business and Labour, Australian National University. These include a variety of newspaper clippings, photographs, advertisement 'block pulls', cycle journals, price lists, and Dunlop's 'Cycling and Motoring Notes'. While many important items relating to the early history of Dunlop in this country have not survived, anyone interested in the development and use of tyres, cycles, motor vehicles or rubber products in Australia will probably find something of interest in the collection.

I sought information from and about former rural cyclists through an appeal in numerous newspapers, eliciting some two hundred replies. I also conducted a series of oral interviews, a number of which are now on deposit in the National Library of Australia, which provided recording equipment. The opinions and experiences personally conveyed by former bush cyclists provided a perspective on the use of the bicycle this century—and some important insights into bush cycling—that could not have been obtained any other way. It is fair to say this study could not have been completed without them. Among those who gave generously of their time and furnished valuable information (although they did not always realise it!) were: ACT: D. Bell, X. Herbert; NSW: W.: H. Bath, W. Beer, A. Carr, R. Faulkner, A.M. Fergusson, B.D. Fisher, B. Goodwin, W. Jacobs, L. Kelly, Y. Leveringham, H.M. Leithead, L.V. Lord, V. Morris, L. Nicholson, R. O'Brien, J. Short, G. Stewart, S.H. Strange, L. Tarrant, B. Watson, P. Wheatley, T. Williams; Qld: D. Harries, E. Hogan, R.E. Little, J. Smith; SA: P. Baillie, H.G. Doecke, P.M. Edge, P.P. Farley, G. Jones, J.M. Keatley, I. McTaggart, R.W. Reichstein, E.J. Rosenzsweig, G. Tomlinson; Tas.: D.J. Atkins, G. Berry, H.J.H. Lade, M.G. O'Dea, M. Schroeter; Vic.: B. Curtis, F.J. Fox, H. Green, R. Harrop, H. Marsh, P. McCallum, A. Richardson, W. Taylor; WA: A. Belford, L. Boulton, F. Broomhall, J. Costello, J.S. Crawford, T. Creasey, M. Durack, J. Easther, F.V. Essex, M. Grant, R.

Gawned, V. Gooding, J. Gould, A. Hartley, B. Hegney, S.J. Hocking, B. Jeffery, B. Jones, H. Jordan, T. Mayman, J. McKenzie, E. Riley, E. Scahill, L. Shepherd, L. Stonehouse, F.H. Tate, S. Trestrail, B. White and L. Witt.

I would like to thank the following for their assistance in the research and preparation of *The Bicycle in Wartime*, from which the Australian materials have been drawn for *Wheeling Matilda*. Cecily Adams, Castlecrag, New South Wales. Donald Berkebile, Donald Kloster, Andrea Stevens and Roger White, of the Smithsonian Institution, Washington, D.C. Staff at the Australian War Memorial, Canberra, including Dr. Michael McKernan, Michael Bogle, Jim Heaton, Michael Piggott, Glynis Vincent, and Peter Stanley. Dr. Brian Bond, Department of War Studies, Kings College, London. Elisabeth Campbell, Phoenix, Arizona. Margaret Chambers, Australian Archives, Brighton, Victoria. Jane Carmichael, Imperial War Museum, London. Gavan Daws, Canberra and Honolulu. Len Deighton, London. Kevin Fewster, Canberra. Gary Fitzpatrick, Geography and Mapping Division, Library of Congress, Washington D.C. B. V. Giuliano, National Roads and Motorists' Association, Sydney. Mrs. Marion Harding, National Army Museum, London. E. S. Holt, Canberra. Ian Jones, Melbourne. R. S. Kohn, Battelle Memorial Institute, Columbus, Ohio. Warren Lennon, Canberra. Greg Lockhart, Senior Research Associate, Faculty of Asian Studies, Australian National University, Canberra. Hugh Lunn, Brisbane. David Marr, Canberra. Sue McKemmish, Australian Archives, Brighton, Victoria. Ian McNeill, Canberra. Ahiromitsu Mori and David Nakamura, Canberra. Sir Hubert Opperman, Melbourne. Thomas Pakenham, London. General Huang Phong, Director, Military History Institute, Hanoi. Rosalind Price, Oxford University Press, Melbourne. Mike Saclier, Noel Butlin Archives of Business and Labour, Australian National University, Canberra, and his staff. Harrison Salisbury, of The New York Times. Sylvie Shaw, ABC Radio, Australia. John Toland, Danbury, Connecticut. Lynn Turner, Professor of History, The Royal Military College, Canberra. Robert Wallace, Sydney. Eric Woolmington, head of the Department of Geography at the Royal Military College, Duntroon.

With respect to the work on *Major Taylor in Australia*, I am grateful to Paul Barron for taking a few moments to glance over my submission to his studio, in mid-1987, appreciating Taylor's significance (though Paul had never heard of him), and deciding that it would make an interesting movie. It was the only unsolicited, over-the-transom project he had ever taken on and it forced me to finally sit down and write my book manuscript for him to work from. It premiered as a two hour movie, *Tracks of Glory*, on the Disney Channel in 1992, and the four hour version premiered four months later on Channel Seven in Australia and won the 1993 Australian Logie Award (their Emmy) as the 'Most Popular Telemovie or Mini-series'.

Those who read the original manuscript include Mel Davies, Honorary Research Fellow in Economic History at the University of Western Australia; Philip Derriman, Sydney Cricket Ground historian; Karen Brown Donovan, Major Taylor's great grand-daughter and keeper of the flame; Michael McKernan, formerly of the University of New South Wales, and a leading light in Australian sports history studies; Peter Nye, author of numerous cycling histories and a doyen of the genre; Andrew Ritchie, prolific cycling historian and Taylor's biographer; Jim Shepherd, historian and member of the Sydney Cricket Ground Museum Task Force; Ronald A. Smith, Emeritus Professor of Exercise and Sport Science at the Pennsylvania State University, and Secretary-Treasurer of the North American Society for Sports History for some 30 years; Frank Van Straten, Hugh McIntosh's biographer; and Bernard Whimpress, former Curator of the Adelaide Oval Museum and Historian of the South Australian Cricket Association.

The foundation for the Major Taylor work was the numerous Australian newspapers, magazines and journals that wrote about him while he was in Australia, already cited above

The other important element was Major Taylor's autobiography, which devoted 150 of its 431 pages to the Australian period alone. It was titled *The Fastest Bicycle Rider in the World: The Story of a Colored Boy's Indomitable Courage and Success Against Great Odds*, and was published by the Wormley Publishing Company, in Worcester, Massachusetts in 1928. I am grateful to the late Sir Hubert Opperman for lending me his copy of the Major's book and talking to me about Taylor. Sir Hubert associated with a number of riders who knew, and had ridden against, the Major and was able to provide me with some valuable observations and comments.

American sources on the Major were scarce prior to 1988. Examples are George Gipe's *The Great American Sports Book* (New York: Doubleday), 1978; Edwin B. Henderson and the editors of Sport magazine, *The Black Athlete: Emergence and Arrival* (New York: Publishers Company Inc.), 1978; John A. Lucas and Ronald A. Smith, *Saga of American Sport* (Philadelphia: Lea & Febiger)1978; and Benjamin G. Rader's *American Sports: From the*

Age of Folk Games to the Age of Spectators (Englewood Cliffs, N. J.: Prentice-Hall), 1983. Richard Mandell, in the April 12th, 1971, issue of *Sports Illustrated*, gave a two-page summary of Taylor's career, in 'The Major Made It on a Bike'. All of those, however, tended to tease rather than satisfy one's curiosity to know more about him.

The turning point was 1988 with Andrew Ritchie's book, *Major Taylor: The Extraordinary Career of a Champion Bicycle Racer* (San Francisco: Bicycle books, Inc.), the first full biography (revised in 2009). It is the basic starting point for future research on him. Also that year, Arthur Ashe, Jr. produced his comprehensive and ambitious work, *A Hard Road to Glory: A History of the African-American Athlete 1619-1918* (New York: Warner Books), in which he devoted four pages to Major Taylor. Peter Nye's *Hearts of Lions: The History of American Bicycle Racing* (New York: W. W. Norton & Company, 1989) is a highly readable historical survey of the history of American bicycle racing and devotes the better part of 20 pages to Major Taylor. Importantly, it also includes substantial material on Floyd MacFarland, including his non-racing roles as manager and promoter. The works of Ashe, Nye and Ritchie introduced Taylor in a way, and on a scale, not previously done in America. It was long overdue and for it they must be thanked.

Background material on Hugh McIntosh, the promoter, was obtained from Chris Cunneen's entry in *The Australian Dictionary of Biography*, Vol. 10, 1891-1939 (Melbourne: Melbourne University Press), 1986; from Richard Broome's article on 'The Australian Reaction to Jack Johnson, Black Pugilist, 1907-9', in Cashman and McKernan's book *Sport in History*, and Frank Van Straten's *Huge Deal: The Fortunes and Follies of Hugh D. McIntosh* (South Melbourne: Thomas C. Lothian), 2004.

Aside from the various works cited above, those wishing a more detailed bibliography can consult *The Bicycle in Wartime* (Brassey's, Washington and London, 1998, or the revised edition, Star Hill Studio, Kilcoy, 2011), and my original PhD thesis 'The Bicycle in Rural Australia: A Study of Man, Machine and Milieu' (copies are in the National Library of Australia and the Australian National University Menzies Library). Between them they list some 1,300 sometimes very obscure sources.

As is the usual declaration, any errors are my own responsibility.

Illustrations

Cover. *New South Wales Motorists' and Cyclists' Annual*, 1905
Preface. La Trobe Collection, State Library of Victoria, LTA 133
2. Western Australian Museum, Perth
4. NSW State Library, DL PX 136 a1972006
6. *Cape Times Weekly Edition*, 25 October 1899
7. Rapidascent
8. State Library of South Australia, Clarendon Collection, B34321
10. George W. Burston and H.R. Stokes, *Round About the World on Bicycles*, Melbourne Bicycle Club, 1890
11. *The Austral Wheel*, January 1898
12. *The Austral Wheel*, September 1896
13. *The Austral Wheel*, May 1897, December 1896, November 1898
14. *Western Mail*, 20 May 1898
16-17. Battye Library, Perth, 5501B/1
19. West Australian Newspapers Limited
20. Western Australian Government Tourist Bureau
21. West Australian Department of Tourism
24. Author's collection
28. Battye Library, 400B/50
31. Jack Costello
32. *Western Argus*, 16 June 1903
34. E.J. Cooke Collection, 31 – 194, Mitchell Library, Sydney
36. William Henry Corkhill Collection, Number 52, National Library of Australia
37, 38. La Trobe Collection, State Library of Victoria, LTA 133
39. *The Austral Wheel*, January 1897
41. E.J. Cooke Collection, 31 – 191, Mitchell Library, Sydney
42, 43. La Trobe Collection, State Library of Victoria, LTA 133
46. Paul Weiss, Division of Plant Industry, C.S.I.R.O., Canberra
49. Battye Library Collection, 5223P, Perth
51. Ted McGowan, Perth, Western Australia
52. *New South Wales Cycling Gazette*, 6 November 1897
53. *Western Mail* 20 May 1898
54. Mr. Gerald O'Dea, Devonport, Tasmania
55. Jerome J. Murif, From Ocean to Ocean, George Robertson & Co., 1897
57. *The Austral Wheel*, March, 1898

58. *Albert MacDonald of Orroroo*, The Austral Cycle Agency, Melbourne, 1898

60. Dunlop Collection, Archives of Business and Labour, Australian National University, Canberra

62. *W.A. Cyclist*, 9 June 1899

64. *WA Wheelman*, 16 December 1898

66. Falk, P3/F, Mitchell Library, Sydney

68. National Library of Australia, pic-vn3302402

69. Author's personal collection

70. State Library of South Australia, Searcy Collection, PRG 280/1/34/335

72. Frank Clune, *Last of the Explorers*, Angus & Robertson, 1942

75. Mrs. Walter Taylor, Canterbury, Victoria

76. Frank Clune, *Last of the Explorers*, Angus & Robertson, 1942

77. The Battye Library, 3679P, Perth

79, 80. Frank Clune, *Last of the Explorers*, Angus & Robertson, 1942

81, 83. Dunlop Collection, Archives of Business and Labour, Australian National University, Canberra

84. *W.A. Cyclist*, 16 June 1899

85. *New South Wales Cycling Gazette*, 19 November 1896

86. Northern Territory Library, Karilyn Brown Collection, Photo no. PH0413/0070

88. Mr. Arnold Carr, Orange, New South Wales

91. Mrs. Mary Schroeter, Longford, Tasmania

92-93. *Sydney Mail*, 6 September 1902

94, 95. *Journal of the Department of Agriculture of Western Australia*, August 1908

96. Ted Creasey, Bicton, Western Australia

97. Len Witt, Coolgardie Western Australia

98. Fred Blakeley, *Hard Liberty*, George Harrap & Co, London, 1938

100, 101. Author's photographs

102. National Library of Australia, nla.pic-vn4600235

103. Dunlop Collection, Archives of Business and Labour, Australian National University, Canberra

105. *The Austral Wheel*, August 1896

106. H. W. Wilson, *With the Flag to Pretoria*, Vol. I, Harmsworth Brothers, London, 1901

107. H.W. Wilson, *After Pretoria*, Vol I, Harmsworth Brothers, London, 1902

108 (both photos). H. W. Wilson, *With the Flag to Pretoria*, Vol. I, Harmsworth Brothers, London, 1901

109. *Cape Times Weekly Edition*, July 30, 1902

111-112. Dunlop Rubber (Australia) Ltd., Noel Butlin Archives, Australian National University, Canberra

116-117. *Cycling*, August 10, 1916

118. Mrs. Cecily Adams, Castlecrag, New South Wales

122. Origin unknown

123. Courtesy of *The Shankei Shimbun*

124. Australian War Memorial, negative number unknown

125. N.R.M.A., *Open Road*, Sydney

126. Malvern Star Bicycles

127. Reproduced in numerous Australian newspapers

128-129. Malvern Star

130-132. Military History Institute, Hanoi

133. Permission of International Publishers Company, Inc. New York.

134. The Battye Library, 5501B/3

137. *New South Wales Cycling Gazette*, 18 June 1898

138. *The Australasian*, 12 December 1896

139. *The Town & Country Journal*, 7 January 1903

140. *The Town & Country Journal*, 14 January 1903

142. La Trobe Collection, State Library of Victoria CB5/6/14/6

145. Adelaide *Chronicle*, 27 February 1904

147. Jeff Groman

148. Jeff Groman

150. Rapidascent

152-153. Tony Lundstrom

155. Humberto Fernandes

156. Alexandra Koutts

158. *The Austral Wheel*, December 1896

162. *The Bulletin*, July 1897

164. Roey Fitzpatrick

166. *The Austral Wheel*, August 1898

167. Jim Fitzpatrick

168. *The Australasian*, 1896

169. Scott Dickason

170. City of Sydney Archives

171. Paul Patterson

173. *Ride On* Magazine

174. Johathan Wherrett

176. Jim Fitzpatrick

178-179. Tim Phillips

Index

Across Australia (film), 68-69
Advocacy for cycling, 174-175
AIS, 151-157
Albert Street, Melbourne, 173
ANZAC Cyclist Battalions, 116-121
ArtBike, 174
AusPost, 167-169
Austral Cycle Agency, 63
Austral Wheel, 11, 12, 13, 37-39, 41-43, 135
Austral Wheel Guide to the Victorian Alps, 41
Austral Wheel Race, 13, 135-136, 138
Australasian Pastoralists' Review, 89, 101
Australia, climate, 4; elevation, 5; population 2
Australian Alps, 10, 40-44
Australian Cycling News, 9
Australian English, 44-47
Australian Institute of Sport, 151-157
Austral Wheel, 138
Australian Legend, 160-163
The Australian Language, 46
Australian Workers' Union Bicycle Corps, 92-93,
Aramac, 89
Armstrong, Lance, 159
Armstrong, Percy, 14-15, 25-26, 105-106
Around Australia rides, 59-63
Baker, Sydney, 46
Barker, Herbert, 98
Battlefronts of Outback, 69
Battye, J.S., 160-161
Bean, C.E.W., *On the Wool Track*, 46; re shearers, 90, 162-163
Bean car, 69
Beijing, 178
Bicycle Federation of Australia, 174
Bicycle Industries Australia, 174

Bicycle Network, 175
Bicycle New South Wales, 174
Bicycle pads, 23; Protection League, 29-33
Bicycles, early technology, 5-6; modern variety, 166; numbers sold, 168
'Bicycling', the concept, 3
Bicycling News, 9
Bike share schemes, 173-174
Birtles, Francis, 66-70
Blockhouses, 107-109
Bloomfield, John, 151
Boer War 3, 6, 61, 67, 104-109
Bourke, 91
Bowcock, Jeff, 100
Brakes, 6, 40, 82, 105
Brindle, J.R. 89
Broadbent, George, road maps, 35, 39;
Broad Arrow Cyclists' Association, 30
Broad Arrow Standard, 30, 33
Bulletin, 90, 161; and White Australia, 141
Bulloo River, 89
Burchett, Wilfred 130-133
Burston, George, round the world ride, 9-10; Victorian Alps 39-40
Carr, AMP, 88
Camels, 4, 5, 18, 21
Camel pads, 6, 27-29
Charleville, 9
Charters Towers, 9, 73
China, electric bikes, 167; number of bicycles, 178
Clarendon, South Australia, 8
Climate, of Australia, 4; of Western Australia, 16
Cloncurry, 89
Coleman, Tom, 59
Coles, Alan 151
Clark, Jackie, 147
Clune, Frank, 71
Collins, Tom, 163
Condobolin, 88

Coolgardie, 17-30, 49-50, 96, 134-136
Coolgardie Cycle Express Co., 25, 27
Cootamundra, 168
Coopers Creek, 89
Copenhagen, 179
Corruption in racing, 138-139
Costello, Jack, 28, 31
Craig, R., 14-15
Crawford, Stewart, 95
Creasey, Ted, 96
Cribb, Doctor, 88
Crowley, Frank, 161
Croydon, 14
Cycle craze, 11-14
Cycle Express services, see 'Cycling telegraph'
Cycle journals and magazines, 13, 33, 37-38, 44, 88, 105
Cycle racing, 12-13; 134-159
Cycling Central (SBS), 157
Cycling Promotion Fund, 175
'Cycling telegraph', 22-27
Cycling Times, 97
Cycling Promotion Fund, 174
Cyclist Battalions, 116-121
Cyclists' Handbook and Guide to the Roads of New South Wales, 37;
Cyclo Sportif, 154-155
Dandaraga Station, 97
Decline of rural use, 98-99
Denning, Jack, 53
Diamond frame, 6, 11
Donald, J., 64
Drought, 4, 18, 74, 99
Drugs, 158-159
Dunlop tyres, 6, 11, 15, 57, 60, 62, 69, 78, 82; 102-103, 109-113
Durack, Patsy, 59
Edward, Alf, 9
1895 Cyclists' and Tourists' Handbook of Victoria, 35

Electric bikes, 167-168
English, Australian and the bicycle, 44-47
Evans, Cadel, 157-158
Festina doping scandal, 159
Fixed wheel, 6
'fixies', 166
Flack, Edwin, 149
Frandsen, Ernie, 97
Freewheel, 6, 82, 166
From Ocean to Ocean, 57
Gambling, 137-139
George Street, 170-171
Gibson Desert, 16
Great Sandy Desert, 16
Goldfields Bicycle Pad Protection League, 29-33
Goullet, Alf, 146-147
Greenwood, Charles, 58
Gulf of Carpentaria, 14, 74
Handlebars, 6, 45, 97, 130, 168
H.E.C. Robinson, 36, 40
Helmets, mandatory wearing, 175-176
High Wheelers, 8-10, 17, 36, 39, 40, 45
Hindhaugh, Jack, 117-121
Home front, Australia, 125-128
Horses and horsemen, 18-21, 43-44, in Boer War, 104-106; in WW I, 115-118; in WW II, 121; 134
Howard, John, 101
Hughenden, 89
Hume Highway, 9
Infrastructure for cycling, 172
Ivanhoe, 91
Jameson's Raid, 104-105
Jenolan Caves, 34
Jerilderie, 91
Kalgoorlie pipeline, and lengthrunners, 96
Kimberley, W.B., 160
Kimberleys, 16
Kramer, Frank, 147
Lawson, Iver, 144-145

Wheeling Matilda

League of Victorian Wheelmen, 39
Lengthrunners, 96
Lonely Lands, 67
Luggage, 6, 59, 82
Lyon, Robert and Francis, 91
MacDonald, Albert, 59
McEwen, Robbie, 158
MacFarland, Floyd, 144-147
Mackay, Donald, 71-80
McNamara, Reggie, 147-148
Major Taylor, 139-146
Malaya-Singapore invasion, 121-124
Malvern Star, 127-129, 149, 168
Marginalisation of cycling, 172
Mather, A.W.B., 58, 62
Meares, Anna, 158
Melbourne Bicycle Club, 9, 136, 138
Melbourne Cricket Ground,
Merritt, John, 160
Military relay rides, 109-113
Motor vehicle ownership, 169-170
Mt Kosciusko, 36
Mulga Bill's Bicycle (poem), 163-165
Murif, Jerome J., 55-57
National Cycling Participation Survey, 171
Narrandera, 91
New Guinea, 78-79
New South Wales Cyclists' Touring Union, 35, 37, 41
New York Times, 148
Niland, Kilmeny and Deborah, 161
Northern Territory Times, 73
N.R.M.A. road service patrol, 125
Nullarbor crossing, 49-53
Nye, Peter, 158-159
Obesity, 170-171
O'Dea, Pat, 53-54
O'Farrell, Major M, 35, 37
O'Grady, Stuart, 157
Olympics, 149-150, 157

On the Wool Track, 46, 163
Oodnadatta, 58
Opperman, Hubert, 65, 144
Orange, 88
Orica-GreenEDGE, 159
Overlanders, 48-87, role, 62-65
Paterson, A.B. 'Banjo', 161-165
Pedal wireless, 102
Penny-farthings 8-10
Pearson, Joseph, 11; and road maps 35-40; ascent of Mt Kosciusko, 36, 44.
Pearson's Weekly, 97
Photography, outback, 67-68, 82-85
Porteous, J., 64
Pneumatic tyre, 5, 9, 11, 15, 34, 60, 102-103, 109-113
Population, 2, 5, 18, 22, 73, 125, 135, 151
Queensland Imperial Bushmen, 106
Rabbits and rabbit fence, 92-95
Racing licences, 136
Railway lines, 5, 17; Boer War, 104, 107-109; shearers and, 92
Receivers of Mail Bags, 24
Reichenbach, Eddie, 81-87
Reminiscences Including Cycling Experiences, 37
Review of Reviews, 35
Richardson, Arthur, 49-50, 59-62, 106
Road Maps, 35-40
Round About the World on Bicycles, 9
Ryko, Ted, 81-87
Safety bicycle, 5, craze, 11-14
Salisbury, Harrison, 133
Semmler, Clement, 161
Serpolette, Mademoiselle, 135,137
Shed Hands' Agreement, 91
Shearers, 90-92
Shearing machine, 101
Singapore, invasion of, 121-124
Snell, William, 50
Snowy Mountains,

Sorenson, E.S., 90
Southern Cross, 17, 18, 25-26
Speedwell, 168
Stainburn Downs, 89
Stewart, C., 89
Stimulants in racing, 159
Stokes, H.R., 9-10
Strawberry picker, 100-101
Strzelecki Track, 92
Such is Life, 163
Swimming, Olympic medals 149-151
Sydney Bicycle Club, 9
Sydney Cricket Ground, 4, 135-136, 140, 141
Sydney Mail, 161
Sydney Morning Herald, 163
Sydney Thousand, 141
Taylor, Major, 139-146
Telegraph lines, in WA, 26-30, 50, 77; Central Australia, 59; the Nullarbor, 65
Tennis Grand Slams, 150
'The Bicycle's Gone to the Bush' (poem), 90
The Story of a Remarkable Ride, 60
Thorn Proof tyre, 103
Tibooburra, 91
Timber cutting, 98
Tolga, 100
Touring Guides, 35-40
Traegar, Alfred, 102
Tsuji, Masanobu, 122-123
Tyres, see pneumatic
Union Cycliste Internatianl (UCI) 157
Velocipede, 8, 45
Velodromes, 154
Vietnam, 129-133
Virgin, William, 52
W.A. Cycling Club, 9
Wagner, Honus, 140
Walker, Don, 139
War cycles, 108-109

Westral Wheel Race, 134-136, 144, 154
White, Alex, 71-78
White, Frank, 53, 71-78
White Australia Policy, 141
Wilcannia, 91
Wilgena, 89
Wimmera, 89
Winton, 89
Witt, Len, 97
World War I, 114-121
World War II, 121-129
Wright, Scotchy, 53
Yanco, 91
Yilgarn Plateau, 16, 19
Zimmerman, Arthur, 135

About the Author

Jim Fitzpatrick grew up in Southern California, graduating from UCLA. After serving with the Peace Corps in El Salvador, he moved to Australia where he has spent most of his adult life and professional career. He earned a PhD in Human Sciences at The Australian National University.

He has been director of Major Gifts for the Salvation Army in Phoenix, Arizona; Executive Administrator of the Australian Spinal Research Foundation; Project Director for a National Library of Australia Oral History Project; Research Officer with the Education Department of Western Australia; an urban planner in southern California; and has taught in the Geography Departments of the Universities of Natal, Western Australia, and New England.

As well as his books on cycling, he is the author of numerous articles and reports on health, education, urban planning and history. The Australian Logie Award-winning film, 'Tracks of Glory', was based on his book, *Major Taylor in Australia*.

Jim and his wife Roey now live in rural Queensland.

The Bicycle and the Bush by Jim Fitzpatrick

The Bicycle and the Bush, cited in the Judges' Report of the 1981 Australian National Book Council Awards, is a superbly illustrated study of the widespread use of the bicycle in the vast Australian Outback by rural workers from 1890 into the 20th century.

The Bicycle in Wartime (Revised Edition) by Jim Fitzpatrick

The Bicycle in Wartime is a landmark work in the field of military history. Complemented throughout with an extensive collection of archival photographs, maps and early book, newspaper and magazine illustrations, this edition has been revised to include new text and photographs and additional material on 21st century military cycle technology.

Major Taylor in Australia by Jim Fitzpatrick

Marshall W. (Major) Taylor, a brilliant black American cyclist of the 1890s and early 20th century, was for some years the highest paid and most famous athlete in what was then the world's most popular and lucrative sport. But he had to battle racial intolerance, dangerous and dirty tactics, and self-serving promoters, and it was in White Australia, in 1904 that it came to a head.

This is the first significant new work on Major Taylor since Andrew Ritchie's original biography in 1988, and includes an excellent collection of photographs, some never before seen in American or Australian books.

www.starhillstudio.com.au

www.ingramcontent.com/pod-product-compliance
Lightning Source LLC
Chambersburg PA
CBHW081224170426
43198CB00017B/2707